DEMOCRACY AND DEVELOPMENT IN AFRICA

Claude Ake

DEMOCRACY AND DEVELOPMENT IN AFRICA

THE BROOKINGS INSTITUTION
Washington, D.C.

HC
800
A648
1996

Library of Congress Cataloging-in-Publication data

Ake, Claude.
  Democracy and development in Africa / Claude Ake.
p. cm.
  ISBN 0-8157-0220-5.—ISBN 0-8157-0219-1
  1. Africa—Economic conditions—1960–   2. Africa—Economic
policy.
  3. Pressure groups—Africa   4. Economic development—Political
aspects. 5. Africa—Politics and government—1960–   6.
Democracy—Africa. 7. Africa—Colonial influence. I. Title.
HC800.A648   1996
339.96—dc20

95-32540
CIP

9 8 7 6 5 4 3 2 1

The paper used in this publication meets the minimum requirements
of the American National Standard for Information Sciences—Perma-
nence of Paper for Printed Library Materials, ANSI Z39-48-1984.

Typeset in Garamond

Composition by Monotype Composition Company, Inc.
Baltimore, Maryland

Printed by R. R. Donnelley and Sons Co.
Harrisonburg, Virginia

℔ THE BROOKINGS INSTITUTION

The Brookings Institution is an independent organization devoted to nonpartisan research, education, and publication in economics, government, foreign policy, and the social sciences generally. Its principal purposes are to aid in the development of sound public policies and to promote public understanding of issues of national importance.

The Institution was founded on December 8, 1927, to merge the activities of the Institute for Government Research, founded in 1916, the Institute of Economics, founded in 1922, and the Robert Brookings Graduate School of Economics and Government, founded in 1924.

The Board of Trustees is responsible for the general administration of the Institution, while the immediate direction of the policies, program, and staff is vested in the President, assisted by an advisory committee of the officers and staff. The by-laws of the Institution state: "It is the function of the Trustees to make possible the conduct of scientific research, and publication, under the most favorable conditions, and to safeguard the independence of the research staff in the pursuit of their studies and in the publication of the results of such studies. It is not a part of their function to determine, control, or influence the conduct of particular investigations or the conclusions reached."

The President bears final responsibility for the decision to publish a manuscript as a Brookings book. In reaching his judgment on the competence, accuracy, and objectivity of each study, the President is advised by the director of the appropriate research program and weighs the views of a panel of expert outside readers who report to him in confidence on the quality of the work. Publication of a work signifies that it is deemed a competent treatment worthy of public consideration but does not imply endorsement of conclusions or recommendations.

The Institution maintains its position of neutrality on issues of public policy in order to safeguard the intellectual freedom of the staff. Hence interpretations or conclusions in Brookings publications should be understood to be solely those of the authors and should not be attributed to the Institution, to its trustees, officers, or other staff members, or to the organizations that support its research.

Foreword

Over the past three decades, Africa's preoccupation with development has had only marginal success. Most Africans are worse off than they were, health and nutrition problems are widespread, and infrastructure is eroding. Many studies have suggested causes for these problems: colonialism, corruption, insufficient technical assistance, unfavorable terms of trade, inadequate entrepreneurial skills, and incompetent management, among others. But Claude Ake believes that political conditions are the greatest obstacle to development.

In most of Africa, colonial rule left a legacy of intense commitment to independence but few ideas regarding appropriate economic policies. Immediately after the new nations achieved independence, the political environment was hostile to development. The internal struggle for power was the absolute focus of attention. But the new leaders soon realized that they needed some new legitimizing theme to replace liberation ideology, and they settled on economic development as a natural alternative. With sparse resources of their own to work with, however, they looked to foreign powers to finance their aspirations and thereby reintroduced in the economic context some of the issues of dependence that they had settled in the political context.

Ake gives an overview of the development policies that have ensued and documents the pattern of failure. He examines the alternatives that can be considered: economic development based on traditional agriculture, political development based on decentralization of power, and reliance on indigenous communities to provide some refuge from the centralized state. His purpose is to outline the fundamental redesign he believes will be necessary.

Claude Ake is director of the Centre for Advanced Social Science in Port Harcourt, Nigeria. He completed this manuscript during his fellowship term as a visiting scholar with the Africa Project at the Brookings

Institution. Earlier versions of this manuscript were read by Robert Berg, Coralie Bryant, and Miguel Schloss. Brookings is grateful to them for their comments and suggestions.

The manuscript was edited by Caroline Lalire and Deborah Styles and verified by Andrew Solomon and Diane Chido. Judy Buckelew, Stacey Seaman, and Louise Skillings prepared the manuscript for publication. Carlotta Ribar proofread the book, Susan Woollen prepared it for typesetting, and Robert E. Elwood prepared the index. Partial funding for this project was provided by the Carnegie Corporation of New York, the Rockefeller Brothers Fund, and the Rockefeller Foundation. Brookings gratefully acknowledges their support.

The views expressed in this book are those of the author and should not be ascribed to the people whose assistance is acknowledged above, to the organizations that supported the project, or to the trustees, officers, or staff members of the Brookings Institution.

MICHAEL H. ARMACOST
President

November 1995
Washington, D.C.

Contents

1

The Development Paradigm and Its Politics

Three decades of preoccupation with development in Africa have yielded meager returns. African economies have been stagnating or regressing. For most Africans, real incomes are lower than they were two decades ago, health prospects are poorer, malnourishment is widespread, and infrastructure is breaking down, as are some social institutions.

Many factors have been offered to explain the apparent failure of the development enterprise in Africa: the colonial legacy, social pluralism and its centrifugal tendencies, the corruption of leaders, poor labor discipline, the lack of entrepreneurial skills, poor planning and incompetent management, inappropriate policies, the stifling of market mechanisms, low levels of technical assistance, the limited inflow of foreign capital, falling commodity prices and unfavorable terms of trade, and low levels of saving and investment. These factors are not irrelevant to the problem. Alone or in combination they could be serious impediments to development.

However, the assumption so readily made that there has been a failure of development is misleading. The problem is not so much that development has failed as that it was never really on the agenda in the first place. By all indications, political conditions in Africa are the greatest impediment to development. In what follows I consider how African politics has been constituted to prevent the pursuit of development and the emergence of relevant and effective development paradigms and programs.

The Political Legacy of Colonialism

To understand this phenomenon, one must begin with colonialism and its political legacy. Colonialism in Africa was markedly different from the

1

colonial experiences of the Americas, Europe, and Asia. To begin with, it was unusually statist. The colonial state redistributed land and determined who should produce what and how. It attended to the supply of labor, sometimes resorting to forced labor; it churned out administrative instruments and legislated taxes to induce the breakup of traditional social relations of production, the atomization of society, and the process of proletarianization. It went into the business of education to ensure that workers could do the jobs they were required to perform and would remain steadfast in the performance of their often tedious and disagreeable tasks. It built roads, railways, and ports to facilitate the collection and export of commodities as well as the import of manufactured goods. It sold commodities through commodity boards. Indeed, it controlled every aspect of the colonial economy tightly to maintain its power and domination and to realize the economic objectives of colonization.

Since the colonial state was called upon by the peculiar circumstances of the colonial situation to carry out so many functions—indeed to do everything—it was all powerful. It needed to be all powerful not only to carry out its mission but also to survive along with the colonial order in the face of the resentment and the hostility of the colonized, a hostility that occasionally broke out into rebellions such as the Mau Mau insurrection in Kenya.

The power of the colonial state was not only absolute but arbitrary. For instance, the colonial governments made the colonies produce the commodities they needed. When the Gold Coast (now Ghana) was colonized, it did not farm cocoa. The colonial government decided that the country would be suitable ground for farming cocoa and duly introduced the crop. In 1865 the country started exporting cocoa, and by 1901 it was the leading producer of the commodity in the world. It quickly became a monocultural cocoa economy; by 1939 cocoa accounted for 80 percent of the value of its exports. In Kenya, the Coffee Plantation Registration Ordinance of 1918 forbade the growing of coffee, the country's most profitable commodity, by Africans. The purpose was to make Africans available for wage labor by keeping them from becoming independent producers as well as to prevent them from stealing coffee from European farms by ensuring they could not legally possess coffee. Other examples of arbitrariness include the reservation of the White Highlands in Kenya for European farmers and the Marketing of Native Produce Ordinance of 1935, which restricted wholesale marketing to Europeans and barred Africans.

These two features of state power, its absolutism and its arbitrariness, framed colonial politics. As if to underscore the arbitrariness of the power of the colonial state, its officials showed hardly any interest in transforming domination into hegemony, beyond the notion that their domination was also a civilizing mission. The colonial situation was not unlike Hobbes's prepolitical state, in which all claims are arbitrary and all rights are only powers. In the essentially military situation of imposing and maintaining colonial domination, the colonizers had no choice but to reject in principle any restrictions on their use of power. There may have been circumstances in which the use of state power was not arbitrary in practice, but it was always arbitrary in principle.

Since the colonial state was for its subjects, at any rate, an arbitrary power, it could not engender any legitimacy even though it made rules and laws profusely and propagated values. Accordingly, in struggling to advance their interests, the colonial subjects did not worry about conforming to legality or legitimacy norms. Colonial politics was thus reduced to the crude mechanics of opposing forces driven by the calculus of power. For everyone in this political arena, security lay only in the accumulation of power. The result was an unprecedented drive for power; power was made the top priority in all circumstances and sought by all means. As the rulers and subordinates extended their rights to their powers, the idea of lawful political competition became impossible, and politics was inevitably reduced to a single issue: the determination of two exclusive claims to rulership. This politics hardly encouraged moderation and compromise.

The Postcolonial Situation

Although political independence brought some change to the composition of the state managers, the character of the state remained much as it was in the colonial era. It continued to be totalistic in scope, constituting a statist economy. It presented itself as an apparatus of violence, had a narrow social base, and relied for compliance on coercion rather than authority.

With few exceptions, the gaining of independence was not a matter of the nationalists' marshaling forces to defeat colonial regimes. More often than not, it was a matter of the colonizers' accepting the inevitable and orchestrating a handover of government to their chosen African successors, successors who could be trusted to share their values and be attentive to their interests. This approach did not succeed in all places where the decolonization was peaceful, much less where it was occasioned by revolutionary struggle. But on the whole, political independence in Africa was rarely the heroic achievement it was made out to be; it was often a convenience of deradicalization by accommodation, a mere racial integration of the political elite.

The tendency to reproduce the past was reinforced by the dispositions of the dominant social forces in the postcolonial era. None of them apparently had any serious interest in transformation, and all of them were only too aware that they could not afford to broaden the social base of state power. What changed over time was the proliferation and intensification of conflict within the nationalist coalition. Class conflict became more salient with the indigenization of the political elite and matured rapidly. It was deepened by the inevitable depoliticization of the nationalist movement to contain frustrations arising from the failure to effect the societal transformation that many had hoped for and fought for. As is clear from many speeches and writings of nationalist leaders, such as Kwame Nkrumah's "I Speak for Freedom," A. A. Nwafor Orizu's "Renascent Africa," and Jomo Kenyatta's "Facing Mount Kenya," the language of nationalism had been radical, propounding distributive, egalitarian, and democratic values.

The nationalist movement was essentially a coalition of disparate groups united by their common grievances against colonial oppression. It was typically a network of nationalities, ethnic groups, religious organizations, syncretistic movements, secondary organizations, and professional interest groups.[1] But even though they cooperated against the colonial regime, their relationship was never free from tension and conflict.

As the prospects for political independence improved, the solidarity of the movement grew weaker and competition between its component units became more intense. Although the members of the coalition fought against the colonial power, they worried about the enormous power they were trying to wrestle from it, power they could not entrust to any one of them or even share in a way that could reduce political anxiety. The normative, institutional, and ideological mechanisms that would have made this power subject to constitutional constraints and accountability did not yet exist. So while agitating to overthrow the colonial regime, the constituent elements of the coalition were also trying to block one another from appropriating it. Increasingly their attention turned from the colonial regime to one another, and eventually the competition among these

1. Coleman (1958).

groups came to dominate political life, while the colonial power, now resigned to the demise of colonialism, became a referee rather than the opponent.

By the time independence was achieved in the early 1960s, the centrifugal tendencies had grown strong enough in many countries (for instance, Nigeria, Kenya, Ghana, Ivory Coast, Sierra Leone, Zambia, Uganda, Cameroon, and Zaire) to threaten not only the transition to independence but, more important, the political viability of the new governments. In trying to deal with these forces of disunity, some African countries, like Nigeria, came to independence with such complex constitutions that systemic breakdown was inevitable.

But for the purpose here, which is to understand the postcolonial state and the politics associated with it, what is pertinent is not so much centrifugalism as the political competition arising from the mutual alienation of the coalition partners. As they pulled apart, they placed more value on capturing political power for themselves and grew increasingly fearful about what seemed to them to be the grave consequences of losing to their rivals in the competition for the control of state power. Thus the premium on political power rose higher and higher and with it the intensity of political competition and its domination by efficiency norms.

The political leaders, too, were exposed to new conflicts. The increasing competition and conflict among nationalities, ethnic groups, and communal and interest groups was reflected in their ranks. They also tended to separate along those lines; indeed, many of them had sought power by politicizing national, ethnic, and communal formations. Now in office, some of them manipulated ethnic and communal loyalties as a way to deradicalize their followers and contain the emerging class division of political society, which could isolate and destroy them. So they began to place emphasis on vertical solidarities across class lines. In particular, they tried to establish mutual identity and common cause by appealing to national, ethnic, communal, and even religious loyalties.

In doing so, they weakened the solidarity of the people, at a great cost. They created not only strong divisions within their own ranks but strong antipathies and exclusivity in society. As always, the exclusivity of the competing political formations increased the premium on political power and the intensity of political competition.

Political intensity was further reinforced by the tendency to use state power for accumulation. This practice was associated with the weak material base of the new political leaders, who had been economically marginalized by the discriminatory economic policies of the colonial regime. Even when they came to power, they had little experience of entrepreneurial activity and little or no capital. Invariably they were obliged to explore the one leverage they had: control of state power to strengthen their material base.

The need for a more secure material base drove the indigenous elite to increase the statism of the economy. An increasing range of economic activities was brought under the control of the state, notably by nationalization, to facilitate the appropriation of wealth by means of state power. The use of state power for accumulation, associated as it is with statism, monopoly power, and the interposition of coercion in the labor process, raised to new heights the premium on the capture of state power.

Finally, political intensity received additional impetus from the alienation of leaders from followers in the postcolonial era. Basically the political elite dealt with the tide of popular discontent arising from the deradicalization of the nationalist movement by enforcing political conformity through coercion. Coercion was used to constrain the political expression of the masses, now disillusioned with the performance of their leaders. Coercion was also used to impose "political unity" in the midst of considerable social pluralism, which had become very divisive for being politicized and exploited by competing elites.

The dominant faction of the political elite found itself utterly isolated, increasingly relying on violence, at war with the rest of society and with rival factions among its own ranks. Political competition now assumed the character of warfare and paved the way for the ascendancy of the specialists of violence, the military. The rash of military coups that came later essentially formalized a reality that was already firmly established. It was not the military that caused military rule in Africa by intervening in politics; rather, it was the character of politics that engendered military rule by degenerating into warfare, inevitably propelling the specialists of warfare to the lead role.

To recapitulate, at independence the form and function of the state in Africa did not change much for most countries in Africa. State power remained essentially the same: immense, arbitrary, often violent, always threatening. Except for a few countries such as Botswana, politics remained a zero-sum game; power was sought by all means and maintained by all means. Colonial rule left most of Africa a legacy of intense and lawless political competition amidst an ideological void and a rising tide of disenchantment with the expectation of a better life.

The Implications of Politics

It is easy to see that the political environment at independence was profoundly hostile to development. The struggle for power was so absorbing that everything else, including development, was marginalized. Those who were out of power constantly worried about their exposure to every kind of assault by a state that was hardly subject to any constitutional or institutional restraints. Since what mattered in this type of politics was the calculus of force, the out-of-power elites strove constantly to put together a credible force to challenge those in power, or, at any rate, to limit their own vulnerability to harassment and abuse. In a highly statist postcolonial polity, they did not even have the option of channeling their ambitions into economic success, which was primarily a matter of state patronage. To become wealthy without the patronage of the state was likely to invite the unpleasant attention of those in control of state power. Political power was everything; it was not only the access to wealth but also the means to security and the only guarantor of general well-being. For anyone outside the hegemonic faction of the political elite, it was generally futile to harbor any illusions of becoming wealthy by entrepreneurial activity or to even take personal safety for granted. For anyone who was part of the ruling faction, entrepreneurial activity was unnecessary, for one could appropriate surplus with less risk and less trouble by means of state power.

Besieged by a multitude of hostile forces that their authoritarianism and exploitative practices had engendered, those in power were so involved in the struggle for survival that they could not address the problem of development. Nor could they abandon it. For one thing, development was an attractive idea for forging a sense of common cause and for bringing some coherence to the fragmented political system. More important, it could not be abandoned because it was the ideology by which the political elite hoped to survive and to reproduce its domination. Since development was the justification for rallying behind the current leadership, for criminalizing political dissent, and for institutionalizing the single-party structure, to abandon it would undermine the power strategy of the elite.

The elite responded to this dilemma by making token gestures to development while trying to pass on the responsibility for development to foreign patrons. Thus while African leaders talked about the fragility of political independence and the need to buttress it by self-reliant development, they eagerly embraced economic dependence. In time, this frame of mind led to the conception of development as something to be achieved through changes in the vertical relations between Africa and the wealthy countries: a greater flow of technical assistance to Africa, more loans on better terms, more foreign investment in Africa, accelerated transfer of technology, better prices for primary commodities, greater access to Western markets, and so forth.

In this spirit, African governments expected a large portion of their development budget to be financed externally. That was true even for those countries such as Tanzania whose leaders seemed conscious of the need for self-reliance. For instance, Tanzania's first postindependence plan of 1964, the first phase of an ambitious fifteen-year development plan, projected an expenditure of $285.7 million for the plan period, of which $222.7 million, or 78 percent, was to come from external sources.

The Development Paradigm

The new leaders of independent Africa knew that to hold on to their power and to divert their people from demands for redistribution and for the structural transformation of the colonial economy, they had to find something to replace the nationalist ideology of self-government, something that would, they hoped, create a sense of common purpose. In the end, they settled for the ideology of development. How did that come about?

Commitment to development, however vaguely conceived, was already implicit in the ideology of the nationalist movement. Without exception, all the nationalist leaders believed that one important lesson to be learned from the humiliation of colonization was the need to overcome not only political weaknesses but also military, economic, and technological ones. The writings of such leaders as Leopold Senghor of Senegal, Nnamdi Azikiwe of Nigeria, Julius Nyerere of Tanzania, Amilcar Cabral of Guinea-Bissau, and Jomo Kenyatta of Kenya expressed the urgent need for African societies to become more competitive in the modern state system, a need often crudely expressed as "catching up with the West."

At the same time, the former colonial masters were also promoting the idea of development. For when the rising tide of nationalism showed that colonialism could not survive, they had contrived the concept of partnership in development to maintain a presence and some leverage in the colonies and to gain allies in the battle against communism.

In this supportive international environment, African leaders adopted the ideology of development to replace that of independence. But as it turned out, what was adopted was not so much an ideology of development as a strategy of power that merely capitalized on the objective need for development. African leaders, such as Kenyatta and Nyerere, argued that now that independence had been won, the overriding task was development, without which political independence could not be consolidated and African countries would not be able to eradicate the humiliation of colonization. Against the pressure for redistribution, they argued that what was needed was hard work to further development, because the surplus had to be produced before it could be shared. The emphasis was shifted to a dedication to hard work; East African leaders changed the nationalist slogan from Uhuru (freedom) to Uhuru na Kaze (freedom means hard work).

The hard work was to be done literally in silence; the overriding necessity of development was coupled with the overriding necessity for obedience and conformity. African leaders insisted that development needs unity of purpose and the utmost discipline, that the common interest is not served by oppositional attitudes. It was easy to move from there to the criminalization of political opposition and the establishment of single-party systems.

The ideology of development was exploited as a means for reproducing political hegemony; it got limited attention and served hardly any purpose as a framework for economic transformation. Of course, development plans were written and proclaimed. But what passed for development plans were aggregations of projects and objectives informed by the latest fads of the international development community such as import substitution and export promotion. As these fads changed in the larger world, so they were abandoned in Africa.

The ideology of development itself became a problem for development because of the conflict between its manifest and latent functions. The conflict is apparent in the actions of African leaders who proclaimed the need for development and made development the new ideology without necessarily translating it into a program of societal transformation. They did so not because they were uninterested in societal transformation but because their minds were absorbed in the struggle for power and survival.

In the end it fell to the West to supply a development paradigm. What was supplied was a more specific form of a broader Western model of social transformation; namely, modernization theory.[2] Modernization

2. Hagen (1962); Lerner (1958); Moore (1963); Levy (1952).

theory was a complex unity of diversities. Some theorists looked at modernization in broad social terms,[3] and some from a political standpoint.[4] Others looked at it from an economic perspective, in which case the periodicity and the evolutionary approach that are a conspicuous element of modernization theory were less so.[5]

In its most common form, modernization theory posits an original state of backwardness or underdevelopment characterized by, among other things, a low rate of economic growth that is at least potentially amenable to alteration through the normal processes of capital. This original state of backwardness is initially universal. According to the theory, the industrialized countries have managed to overcome it. All the other countries could conceivably overcome backwardness too if they adopted appropriate strategies. Modernization theory—for instance, Rustow's theory of stages—assumes that progress tends to be spatially diffused, a process by which more and more countries evolve from the state of backwardness, capitalizing on the experience of those that developed before them. The spatial distribution of progress, however skewed at any time, is not static but dynamic. By proximity and interaction, progress is diffused through space. Progress, or modernity, by its very nature is apt to strain beyond its locus, overflowing into the adjacent space and transforming it. Thus uneven development is a transitional phenomenon that can be removed sooner or later by creating certain favorable conditions within the underdeveloped regions and by ensuring the appropriate interactions between them and the developed regions.

Without exception, modernization theory used an evolutionary schema that regarded the ideal characteristics of the West as the end of social evolution. This meant that, reduced to essentials, the development of the backward parts of the world was also implicitly a matter of becoming Western. But since the theorists viewed development, not westernization (that was only implicit), as a state of being that is objectively good and universally desirable, they did not seem culturally biased. When modernization theory came in conflict with the divergent social structures in the third world, the modernization theorists talked simply of making the structure of the backward country identical to Western ones. When the theorists encountered cultural resistance, they proclaimed the need for the modernization of attitudes. As a result, the theory did not come to terms with the historical specificities of backward countries.

3. See, for instance, Rustow (1960; 1971); Apter (1965); Lerner (1958)
4. See, for instance, Shils (1962); Organski (1965).
5. Hirschman (1958); Heilbroner (1963); Bauer and Yamey (1957).

In the version of modernization theory applied to Africa, such as W. W. Rustow's *Stages of Economic Growth* (1960), development replaces modernization, the state of backwardness is regarded as preindustrial, the movement to overcome it becomes the process of economic growth to be engineered by neoclassical tools, and the end of social evolution—that is, modernity—means industrialization and high mass consumption. In the postwar period, when the development of the third world came into vogue, development thinking leaned more toward John Maynard Keynes than toward the classical tradition. By the late 1950s the orientations and assumptions of development thinking had become more structuralist.

The development paradigm was initially characterized by a distrust of the price mechanism and an interest in aggregate variables and the interventionist role of the state. The general concern was how the growth of national income could be facilitated by the state and how aggregate variables could be manipulated, especially in the manner of the Harrod-Domar model. Influential economists such as Ragnar Nurske saw development and growth largely as a matter of industrialization. Some could not quite distinguish between industrialization and development; others such as Rustow confused both with westernization. Attention was focused on increasing the wealth of the nation rather than on the welfare of people, a focus shared by most African leaders, such as Nkrumah and Kenyatta, who were concerned about catching up with the West.

One might talk of a second phase in development thinking beginning in the 1970s, when structuralism came under pressure for emphasizing industrialization to the neglect of agriculture, and national wealth to the neglect of welfare. In the light of the criticisms, more attention was paid to such social issues as employment, income distribution, and rural development. This change was officially recognized by the United Nations when it proclaimed the 1970s as the second United Nations development decade. However, the change was only superficial. Behind the veneer of a new critical awareness, the reduction of development to economic growth and a decidedly neoclassical notion of economic growth continued.

Strangely, the neoclassical paradigm prevailed and was not seriously questioned even as African economies continued to deteriorate. The growth rate in the manufacturing sector, which was 8.5 percent in 1960-65, declined to 3.6 percent in 1980-81 and to 0.4 percent in 1982-83. The growth rate of the mining sector, which was 18.5 percent in 1965, fell to −13.2 percent in 1981-82 and to −24.6 percent in 1982-83. In agriculture, the growth rate declined from 1.4 percent in 1960-65 to 0.4 percent in 1982-83. In the food sector, the growth rate declined from

1.6 percent in 1960–65 to 0.2 percent in 1982–83. Food self-sufficiency ratios dropped from 98 percent in the 1960s to 86 percent in 1980.[6]

One would have expected the poor performance of African economies to have undermined confidence in the received neoclassical paradigm. But far from being undermined, the validity of the paradigm was asserted so aggressively that the prospect of using another paradigm could no longer be seriously entertained. For as African economies declined, they became more vulnerable and more dependent on the international development agencies, whose response to Africa's worsening crisis was to affirm the old paradigm in a more doctrinaire form.

Implications of the Paradigm

The development paradigm was severely limited by the political interests that produced it, interests that were often in conflict with the quest for development. One significant limitation was that the paradigm conceives development as an autonomous process, independent of politics, culture, and institutional framework. Conceiving development in this way allowed the African leadership unrestricted liberties. They could appropriate selectively from African traditional institutions and culture, using what served them best to maintain and exploit power and discarding the rest. Thus they used traditional institutions and notions of consensus to justify one-party systems without drawing attention to the traditional processes of consultation and participation that produced this consensus.

For the foreign patrons of Africa, this conception of development offered the advantage of dehistoricizing development, so that it was easier to represent their values and experience as objectively desirable and inevitable. Furthermore, their power and legitimacy as agents of development are associated with their scientific knowledge of the development process, knowledge that is less prone to being questioned when the development process is regarded as autonomous.

In trying to protect their knowledge of the development process from being questioned or made relative, the theorists and agents of development greatly compromised its scientific value. For by regarding development as an autonomous process, they became indifferent to important issues of scientific, epistemological, and ontological significance, issues arising from development's historical origins as a body of knowledge. They could

6. Organization of African Unity (1986, p. 5).

no longer be sensitive to the questions of why development lore made certain assumptions, used certain concepts, valued certain aspects of experience and not others, focused on certain issues and ignored others, and how it adopted a particular discursive practice and particular strategies for ordering experience. In effect, they committed themselves to an abstract science of development rather than to an applied science. If they had posited the necessity of an applied science, they would have had a markedly different scientific tool from the one employed with such indifferent results.

Because the development paradigm largely ignored the specificity and historicity of African countries, it put them in a position in which everything was relevant to them and nothing was uniquely significant for understanding them. Hence the mounting anarchy of development studies and development practice in Africa. Bits and pieces borrowed from theories and paradigms constructed for other purposes and other kinds of experience, meaningless for being incomplete and out of context, were applied in ways and for purposes that are not always clear and to realities that defy comparability.

Paradigm and Institutional Framework

The development paradigm suffered greatly from being indifferent to the institutional framework of development. There was little concern about how the political structures and practices, the administrative system, or even the social institutions of a country might affect its possibility of development.

But how could one assume that the development process was independent of the institutional framework? On closer examination it appears that what was assumed was not so much that the institutional framework did not matter as that there was no need to pay close attention to it. For the importance of the institutional framework is clearly evident in the development paradigm. The paradigm acknowledges the significance of the state, the market, the rule of law, the financial system, employers and employees, associations, and so on. Why then is the paradigm largely indifferent to the institutional framework in Africa? One reason might be the teleologic nature of the paradigm. It is so focused on the state of development and the possibility of development that it fails to pay sufficient attention to the realities on the ground.

Another reason for the indifference might be that it is taken for granted that these African institutions do not vary significantly from their Western forms. This misleading assumption could arise from subtle distortions of the relationship among language, consciousness, and experience, distortions that often arise from ethnocentrism, to which development studies have been prone. People so often mistake the word for the thing. When we use phrases such as the "state in Africa," we immediately give it the content of our own historical experience. Indeed, having named it and given it this content, we feel we have already settled the question of what it is, beforehand. We conflate experience and reality, form and content, because our knowledge is so tied to our language.

This outlook is a particularly serious obstacle to development in Africa. The development paradigm and African development strategies have assumed that the so-called modern sector—the state and its apparatus—is not much different from what it is in the West. The differences are purely subjective factors such as the inefficiency, corruption, and parochialism of officials and the authoritarianism of leaders, differences that could be reconciled eventually by the logic of capitalism.

The similarities are more apparent than real, however. The state in Africa has been a maze of antinomies of form and content: the person who holds office may not exercise its powers, the person who exercises the powers of a given office may not be its holder, informal relations often override formal relations, the formal hierarchies of bureaucratic structure and political power are not always the clue to decisionmaking power. Positions that seem to be held by persons are in fact held by kinship groups; at one point the public is privatized and at another the private is "publicized," and two or more political systems and political cultures in conflict may coexist in the same social formation.

The state-building project and the articulation of the former colonial state with indigenous society have given rise to complex institutional forms. Indigenous society and the modern structures that the state-building project has tried to introduce have been changed, fragmented, and reconstituted in hybrid and unique configurations. Often people do not know whether they are dealing with transitional phenomena or new complex totalities. The feasibility of development strategies and much else besides depends on understanding these changes. Because of them the institutional environment in Africa has become so complicated and so important in determining how people behave that any development paradigm that takes this environment for granted will not be a useful tool for the pursuit of development.

The Cultural Context

Culture, like the institutional framework, has been largely ignored as if it, too, had no serious implications for the success of development strategies. It is easy enough theoretically to discount the cultural factor in the development paradigm. But that has been a costly error. African culture has fiercely resisted and threatened every project that fails to come to terms with it, even as it is acted upon and changed. In the face of this resistance, concerns arose about the need to modernize attitudes and culture, a posture that suggests that the way to deal with cultural resistance is to abolish traditional culture. Instead of looking at traditional culture as something that the development paradigm has to come to terms with and even build on positively, many disdained it.

The more the resistance of African culture became evident, the more the agents of development treated it with hostility; and soon enough, they construed anything traditional, including the rural people, negatively. They castigated peasants for being bound to tradition, for being conservative and suspicious of change, for being irrational, unenterprising, superstitious, and too subjective and emotional in their attitudes. The impression was given that Africans, particularly the rural people, are, by virtue of being themselves, enemies of progress, including their own progress, for it is their own peculiar characteristics that sustain their underdevelopment.

Unfortunately, taking this position makes the people and their culture problematic rather than the process of development itself. By failing to question the development process and the development goal, the development paradigm undermines the scientific value of the concept of development and produces only tautologies and circularities. For the task of scientific investigation is now mainly to assess the possibility of development, a process whose end is already determined in a way that also determines the questions and answers about the inquiry. The country that is developing or developed has the qualities needed for development, and the country that is not developing lacks them; this is what is repeated implicitly over and over again. Everything is true by definition. One never really knows why and how a country is developing or why a country is not developing.

Because the development paradigm tends to have a negative view of the people and their culture, it cannot accept them on their own terms. Its point of departure is not what is but what ought to be. The paradigm focuses on the possibility of Africa's becoming what it is not and probably can never be. Inadvertently perhaps, it discourages any belief in the integrity and the validity of African societies and offers the notion that African societies can find validity only in their total transformation, that is, in their total self-alienation.

On a practical level, the result has been demoralizing. To all appearances some Africans, especially the acculturated, have internalized the paradigm's negative image of themselves as well as notions of the superiority of developed societies. Thus it is often assumed in these circles that foreign-made goods are better, that foreign experts know better, and that the major business of Africa, indeed the only business, is catching up with the industrialized nations. And catching up depends heavily on maintaining relations with these nations and increasing the resource flows from them to Africa. The lack of self-confidence has been obvious in the behavior of many African leaders: Idi Amin's longing for white aides; the submissive behavior of senior officials and even heads of state to relatively minor officials of foreign governments and development agencies; the longing of African leaders for approval in the West; Emperor Jean Badel Bokassa's longing for long-forgotten and better-forgotten French monarchs; and the decision of some African governments to disallow the speaking of African languages and the wearing of African traditional clothes in parliament.

The states of mind that produce such behavior and attitudes cannot be conducive to development. Development requires changes on a revolutionary scale; it is in every sense a heroic enterprise calling for consummate confidence. It is not for people who do not know who they are and where they are coming from, for such people are unlikely to know where they are going.

Conclusion

The political context of the development project has rendered it improbable. In postcolonial Africa the premium on power is exceptionally high, and the institutional mechanisms for moderating political competition are lacking. As a result, political competition tends to assume the character of warfare. So absorbing is the struggle for power that everything else, including the quest for development, is marginalized.

The politics that rendered development improbable has made the adoption of an ideology of development inevitable. For the political elites struggling to maintain their power and to reproduce their domination amid the problems of the postcolonial era, the ideology of development has been an effective strategy of power that addresses the objective necessity for development. The former rulers of Africa eagerly endorsed this ideology, seeing in it the opportunity of a partnership that would allow them to maintain influence in the former colonies and promote their interests in the context of the cold war.

As an ideology, development served a dual function. It represented the interests of the African political elites and their patrons. At the same time, it was an ideology of economic transformation. But the latter was secondary. As a basis for economic change, the ideology was shaped decisively by the essentially political interests of its proponents; hence its many ambiguities and contradictions. Development was regarded as an autonomous process, used to justify whatever powers and liberties the managers of development wanted to give themselves.

When the ideology was eventually formulated as a paradigm of development, a task that the African leaders left to the international development community, the paradigm was conveniently abstract. It paid little heed to historical specificity and treated the development process as something in no way connected to its cultural, institutional, and political context. Again, this position was self serving. For the external patrons of the development paradigm, its abstract universalism allowed them to package their experience as universal and objectively necessary. For African leaders, it secured the liberty to use African culture selectively and opportunistically and to adopt whatever political institutions and practices suited their convenience. The problem was that the qualities that made the development paradigm so functional for those purposes also limited its usefulness as a tool of societal transformation and economic development.

2

A Confusion
of Agendas

In the preceding chapter, I argued that the main obstacle to development in Africa is political, that the point is not so much that the development project has failed as that it never got started in the first place. In what follows, I want to elaborate on that point with reference to the conflict over development agendas between Africa's rulers and the international development agencies.

This conflict has stalled the development project by leaving African leaders trapped in the dilemma of choosing between an endogenous agenda that they cannot find the means to implement and an exogenous agenda that they cannot bring themselves to accept, between what they want to do and what they must do.

Problems of Controlling the Development Agenda

As noted, with independence African leaders were in no position to pursue development; they were too engrossed in the struggle for survival and the need to cope with the many problems threatening their countries and their power. At the same time they could not afford to ignore development, since the quest for it had become their strategy of power as well as the raison d'être of their regimes. Most of them tried to escape from this dilemma by foisting the burden of development on other countries and therefore fell into what has become known as dependent development. It would have been difficult to avoid dependent development in any case because of the integration of African economies into the metropolitan economies during the colonial era. Indeed, the colonies largely derived their structural coherence, limited as it was, from this integration. In themselves, they were structurally disarticulated because they had been developed as aggregations of enclaves, each linked to the metropolitan economy but not necessarily to one another.

That is not to say that dependent development was predetermined by colonialism. The incorporation of African economies into the world capitalist system and the structural constraints associated with it did not entirely preclude the option of self-reliant development. In the final analysis, dependent development was a politically driven decision hinging on considerations of political survival, considerations that impelled African leaders to marginalize development and even their role in its pursuit. It is indicative of their limited commitment to development that with few exceptions, African countries came to independence with hardly any discernible vision of development and no agenda for its realization. Most of the newly independent countries relied heavily on expatriates for their development plans, which were usually collections of policy targets and programs that took for granted the validity of the inherited economic structure.

Manpower shortages, especially the dearth of economists, was part of the problem. Few African countries had a pool of economists to support public policy. Some countries had no universities. In Zambia, where per capita income had been one of the highest at independence, the ratio of expatriates (mostly macroeconomists) to Zambians on the National Commission for Development Planning in 1975 (a decade after independence) was 21 to 4. The Zambians were largely junior, both in qualifications and position. In this respect Zambia was typical. The dearth of native economists and planners led to a reliance on expatriate staff, which in turn caused the reproduction of neocolonial notions of development. Not surprisingly, the first-generation development plans in Africa, such as Kenya's Development Plan, 1964 (the Red Plan), its Development Plan, 1966 (the Green Plan), Tanzania's First Five-Year Development Plan, 1964, and Nigeria's First National Development Plan, 1962–68, simply followed the rhythm of the colonial economy. It would appear, however, that manpower constraints were a minor problem compared with the dearth of ideas and a weak political will.

The poverty of ideas was remarkable. Several countries, such as Ghana, Angola, and Guinea-Bissau, came to independence with an economic agenda, but even there the agenda was largely political. In the end, the international development community provided the development paradigm and agenda for Africa. For the vast majority of African countries, the one thing new in the early years of independence was some concern for indigenizing the public service and giving the local middle class better opportunities to participate in the economy. Even then this concern was more of a reflex action than a doctrine. It was not until 1965 (two years after independence) that the Kenyatta government brought out a paper expressing some rudimentary ideas of development.[1] But this merely rationalized the mixed economy of Kenya.

In Tanzania a vision of development was evident in the Arusha Declaration (1967), which proclaimed African socialism. In Zambia, a vision was evident in President Kenneth Kaunda's philosophy of humanism in his Mulungushi Declaration of 1968. In both instances, these departures, relatively bold by prevailing standards, were essentially reactions to disappointments with the West's lukewarm support. As Zambia's White Paper of 1964 and Tanzania's First Five-Year Development Plan, 1964 indicate, both countries had chosen the capitalist road to development with expectations of massive financial and technical assistance from the West. But those expectations did not materialize.

Zambia and Tanzania, as well as one or two other countries, attempted to regain control of the development agenda but did not succeed. The case of Zambia illustrates the fate of such attempts. Initially Zambia had followed the old-style colonial management of the economy in what has been described as Zambia's "classical neocolonial phase."[2] In the wake of President Kaunda's disillusion with the multinationals, especially the mining companies and Western governments, he made the Mulungushi speech and embarked on indigenization, nationalization, and a "basic needs strategy" that he called humanism. He soon found that the Zambian economy was so dependent that pushing for full control of it by Zambians would be unrealistic. In the end he settled for 51 percent government control of the major corporations.

The mining companies were nationalized under the Zambia Consolidated Copper Mines, later known as the Zambia Industrial and Mining Corporation. In doing so, Zambia incurred a huge debt in compensation payments to foreign shareholders and the hostility of the expatriates who controlled the management, technology, and production in the mines. This hostility forced Zambia to retreat from its ambitious goals to the point that by 1982 the program of indigenization was largely reversed. In the 1970s these problems, along with external shocks and the decline of grade ore reserves, pushed the country to a course of increasing indebtedness and dependence on the World Bank and the International Monetary Fund (IMF). Subsequently Zambia acknowledged the limits of controlling

1. Government of Kenya (1965).
2. Mudera (1984).

its economy and negotiated a series of stabilization programs and standby arrangements with these Bretton Woods institutions: July 1976, April 1978, July 1982, March 1984, January 1985, June 1986, December, 1986.

Unlike Zambia and Tanzania, the vast majority of African countries did not have the political will to attempt to regain control of the development agenda. Most African leaders concentrated on survival and followed the line of least resistance in development strategy. This meant relying on the technical assistance, foreign mission reports, project analyses, and blueprints of international development agencies.[3]

But the complacency of African leaders was short lived; they were soon having problems with leaving policy management to others. In time they recognized emerging differences between their own interests and the concerns of the external development agents. Eventually they began to develop their own ideas about how to proceed, thus paving the way for a conflict of agendas.

Competing Agendas

Nowhere is the conflict more evident than in the rift between the Bretton Woods institutions and African governments over approaches to African development. Even though individual African states seemed content to surrender the development agenda to external development agencies, they did grope collectively, under the auspices of the Organization of African Unity (OAU), toward a vision of how to proceed. The first conference of the heads of state of independent Africa in May 22–25, 1963, adopted a resolution called Areas of Cooperation in Economic Problems. A committee was then set up to study the ideas of a common tariff system to protect Africa's infant industries, a commodities stabilization fund, the freeing of African currencies from external attachments, the restructuring of international trade in Africa's favor, and the harmonization of African development strategies. The view of African development implicit in these concerns is clear enough, and African governments have continued to maintain this view with only minor modifications in emphasis and detail.

The continuity of this perspective on the problems of African economies is evident in subsequent resolutions and position papers of the African states: *Africa's Strategy for Development in the 1970's*, which was adopted by the United Nations Economic Commission for Africa (UNECA, or ECA) Conference of Ministers in Tunisia, February 1971;

3. Among the reports and blueprints that became influential were: for Kenya, ILO (1972), Burrows (1975); for Nigeria, World Bank (1974); for Zambia, ILO (1981).

African Declaration on Cooperation, Development, and Economic Independence, which is also called the Addis Ababa Declaration, a document adopted by the OAU Assembly of Heads of States and Governments in 1973; *The Revised Framework of Principles for the Implementation of the New International Economic Order in Africa*, adopted at Kinshasa in December 1976 by the OAU Council of Ministers and in July 1977 by the OAU heads of states in Libreville; *Monrovia Declaration of Commitment of the Heads of States and Governments of the Organization of African Unity on Guidelines and Measures for National and Collective Self-Reliance in Social and Economic Development for the Establishment of a New International Economic Order*, adopted in July 1979 by the OAU heads of states and governments in Monrovia (the results of a colloquium organized by the OAU and UNECA in February 1979 on the Perspectives of Development and Economic Growth in Africa up to the Year 2000).

Such was the course of the OAU's thinking that culminated in *The Lagos Plan of Action for the Implementation of the Monrovia Strategy for the Economic Development of Africa*, the most comprehensive and systematic statement of the vision of Africa's leaders on the development of Africa. The plan resulted from a decision of the sixteenth assembly of the heads of states and governments of the OAU to hold a special economic summit to find a suitable response to the deepening economic crisis in Africa. The summit, held in April 1980 in Lagos, adopted the plan. The clash between *The Lagos Plan of Action*, which became the classic work on African development strategy, and the World Bank's *Accelerated Development in Sub-Saharan Africa: An Agenda for Action (1981)*, which became the classic perspective of the Bretton Woods institutions on African development, is highly significant.

The Lagos Plan of Action stemmed from the disappointment of African leaders with the continent's economic progress and their conviction that the inadequacy of exogenous development strategies contributed importantly to Africa's poor development record, a view succinctly expressed in the preamble:

The effect of unfulfilled promises of global development strategies has been more sharply felt in Africa than in the other continents of the world. Indeed, rather than result in an improvement in the economic situation of the continent, successive strategies have made it stagnate and become more susceptible than other regions to the economic and social crisis suffered by the industrialised countries. Thus Africa is unable to point to any significant growth rate, or satisfactory index of general well-being, in the past 20 years. Faced with this situation, and determined to undertake measures for the basic restructuring of the economic base of our continent, we resolved to adopt a far-reaching regional approach based primarily on collective self-reliance.[4]

To the irritation of Africa's foreign patrons, *The Lagos Plan of Action* argued that Africa's economic problems were partly caused by Africa's dependence and openness to exploitation; hence the necessity of self-reliance:

Africa is susceptible to the disastrous effects of natural and endemic diseases of the cruelest type and is a victim of settler exploitation arising from colonialism, racism and apartheid. Indeed, Africa was directly exploited during the colonial period and for the past two decades; this exploitation has been carried out through neo-colonialist external forces which seek to influence the economic policies and directions of African States.[5]

The Lagos Plan and the World Bank Study

The Lagos plan was a design for restructuring African economies on two principles: self-reliance (national and collective) and self-sustaining development. Restructuring for self-reliance was to entail, among other things, changing Africa's location in the existing international division of labor, changing the pattern of production from primary commodities to manufactured goods, and relying more on internal sources of raw materials, spare parts, management, finance, and technology. The pursuit of national self-reliance was to be a matter of depending more on internal demand to stimulate production and less on imported inputs. Collective self-reliance would entail collective action to reduce Africa's vulnerability to external forces, a pooling of resources, and greater inter-African trade and cooperation.

The Lagos plan leans toward participative development. It takes a holistic approach in several ways: in treating agriculture and industrial development together and being methodically attentive to the effects of the one on the other, in recognizing the integral relation of the internal and external causes of the African crisis, and in seeing development as a

4. OAU (1982, p. 1).
5. OAU (1982, p. 3).

task that must involve everyone and every sector, private and public, agriculture and industry, labor, capital, and peasantry.

Accelerated Development grew out of a request made by the African governors of the World Bank and the IMF to prepare a study of the economic problems of Sub-Saharan Africa and suggest ways of solving them. The governors were reacting to the *World Development Report, 1972*, which presented a bleak picture of Africa's development prospects. *Accelerated Development* was duly prepared and published in 1981.

The study sees the African crisis as a production crisis in agriculture, particularly in food production. It acknowledges that external factors, especially stagflation in the industrialized countries, high energy costs, and the slow growth of trade in primary commodities, are problems for Africa. However, the emphasis is overwhelmingly on the internal causes of underdevelopment of human resources, climatic conditions and over-production, and policy failures. According to the study, the remedy for Africa's ailing economies lies in giving market forces freer play to bring about dynamism and efficiency. It singles out three areas for attention:

Trade and exchange rate policies, mainly the reduction of import and export duties, subsidies, overvalued exchange rates, and marketing costs.

Reform of input supply and marketing services for agricultural producers. This refers mainly to parastatals, which are to be managed better and made competitive and more in tune with market forces.

More effective use of resources in the public sector. While attention is to be paid to smallholders, it is to be selective, with focus on those areas where physical and human resources promise a higher payoff.[6]

Merely to summarize *Accelerated Development* is to see immediately why it was perceived by Africans to be against their interests. For instance, the study wanted Africa to concentrate on primary production, particularly agricultural products. African leaders, however, felt that a fundamental cause of Africa's problems was precisely its specialization in primary production. In emphasizing production for export, the report was perceived to be reinforcing Africa's dependence on markets that were becoming increasingly hostile and protectionist. African leaders felt that the Bank study glossed over problems that the international economy poses for Africa, problems that are fundamental, though by no means the only cause of Africa's predicament. These include low commodity prices, high interest rates in the West, and the debt burden. But in fairness to the authors of the study and the World Bank itself, it is not so much that they

6. World Bank (1981, p. 5).

dismiss those problems but that they take them as part of the realities on the ground, which need to be minimized and if possible overcome by appropriate policies.

Accelerated Development came to be regarded by some African leaders as a political and ideological document masked as economics that attempts to induce its readers to accept largely false or misleading issues, irrelevant solutions, and a wrong agenda. When the document appeared, a working group from the secretariats of the OAU and the African Development Bank (ADB) and UNECA was set up to examine it. A paper was duly produced and tabled before the African governors of the bank. After studying the paper, the governors decided that the report needed to be further examined and discussed at a meeting to be organized by the ADB, the OAU, and UNECA. The working group of the three organizations resumed work on the report and prepared another paper in January 1982. The paper argued that *Accelerated Development* was analytically defective, disingenuous, and contradictory to African interests, that "the goals, objectives and characteristics of the strategy contained in the report are in many ways inconsistent with those of *The Lagos Plan of Action*."

A more pointed clash of the two viewpoints took place at the eighth meeting of ministers (responsible for economic development and planning) of UNECA at its seventh session in Tripoli in April 1982. The African ministers expressed their evaluation of the report in a document called *Declaration of Tripoli on the World Bank Report Entitled "Accelerated Development in Sub-Saharan Africa: An Agenda for Action."* They argued that "the strategy recommended in the World Bank report, which emphasizes export orientation in general, and primary commodity export in particular, regards industrialization and economic cooperation and integration in Africa as long-term issues and completely disregards external factors as being major constraints on Africa's development and economic growth, that it adopts approaches, concepts and objectives which are divergent from those of *The Lagos Plan of Action* and *The Final Act of Lagos* and opposed to the political, economic and social aspirations of Africa." They went on to "affirm that the goals and objectives defined by African countries for themselves in *The Monrovia Strategy*, *The Lagos Plan of Action*, and *The Final Acts of Lagos* remain the authentic and authoritative goals and objectives for Africa."

The struggle for the development agenda had begun in earnest. The Bretton Woods institutions and the West would not accept the approach of the Lagos Plan, although they refrained from opposing it openly. Instead, they expressed their rejection of the plan by ignoring it and refusing to reorient their economic relations with Africa so as to connect with and address the programs and policies of the plan. That was enough to render the plan inoperable. In the end, African leaders found that they were too dependent and too weak to have their way, and they started to retreat. They talked less about the Lagos plan, they tried to signal their willingness to reform their economies along the lines suggested by the World Bank study, and, most significant, they increasingly adopted structural adjustment programs. But the formal surrender did not occur until July 1985, five years after the launching of the plan, when the Assembly of the Heads of States and Governments of the OAU collectively signaled their defeat.

The clash of agendas again became prominent in the attempt to deal with the economic crisis that had become acute in the early 1980s. The depth of the crisis was documented in the *World Development Report, 1984*: rising infant mortality; food dependence; malnutrition, threatening as many as 100 million people; and so forth.[7]

The report suggested that even with some fundamental improvements in economic management, per capita income would continue its downward trend for the decade 1985–95. In an alternative scenario, which was less optimistic in its assumptions, the report projected GDP growth at 2.8 percent a year, compared with a population growth rate of 3.5 percent a year, for an annual GDP fall of 0.7 percent a year. This meant that 65 to 80 percent of Africa's population would be living below the poverty line by 1995. By 1984 African leaders had recognized that the economic decline of Africa was so deep that it had created a real emergency that had to be addressed urgently and vigorously. Consultations were held among African leaders in the context of organizations such as UNECA, the Economic Community of West African States, the OAU, and the African Development Bank (ADB). At the same time, pressure started to mount for a special session of the UN General Assembly on the African crisis. In Resolution 39/29 of December 3, 1984, the General Assembly drew attention to the "critical economic situation" existing in Africa, and in Resolution 40/40, of December 2, 1985, it agreed to convene a special session to "focus in a comprehensive and integrated manner, on the rehabilitation and medium-term and long-term development problems and challenges facing African countries."[8]

In anticipation of the special session, the African countries prepared a comprehensive document called *Africa's Submission to the Special*

7. World Bank (1984).
8. United Nations (1986).

Session of the United Nations General Assembly on Africa's Economic and Social Crisis.[9] This submission contained an analysis of the African crisis as well as a program of action for getting out of it. It was adopted at the first extraordinary meeting of the UNECA Conference of Ministers on March 28-29, 1986, and the fifteenth extraordinary session of the OAU Council of Ministers in Addis Ababa, March 30-31, 1986. The program of action in the submission, known as Africa's Priority Program for Economic Recovery, 1986-90 (APPER), had been approved by the Assembly of African Heads of States and Governments of the OAU meeting at its twenty-first ordinary session in Addis Ababa, July 18-20, 1985.

According to the submission, APPER was rooted in the Lagos plan, which, it was claimed, had become even more relevant in view of the deepening crisis. Thus the aims of achieving a radical change in the patterns of production and consumption, social and economic structural transformation, and accelerated economic growth and development as well as the integration of the economies of the region, remained of critical importance. APPER translated such broad principles into a sharply focused, practical, and operational set of activities and policies to be implemented during 1986-90 to lay the basis for durable structural change and an improved general level of productivity.[10]

But this claim was misleading, for APPER largely embraces the critical assumptions and the strategies of *Accelerated Development* while discarding those of the Lagos plan. In their struggle to implement the Lagos plan, African leaders had learned the futility of trying to determine the development agenda and trying to carry it out without the cooperation of the West. They saw in clearer relief how weak and dependent they were. The African countries tailored APPER to the World Bank study in order to avoid another clash that they were bound to lose, with perhaps even more disastrous consequences. APPER's concern was much narrower than the structural transformation that it proclaimed. Like *Accelerated Development*, it placed emphasis on Africa's traditional areas of "comparative advantage," especially agriculture, which was now to get 20 percent of total investment. The agricultural sector was now seen as the source of the dynamics of economic development as well as of self-reliance:

In putting special emphasis on the agricultural economy, the Priority program seeks to revitalize the more dynamic and internally based forces for growth and development. The Program recognizes the crucial

9. OAU (1986).
10. OAU (1986, p. 27).

fact that the satisfaction of food requirements for the African people hinges on the rapid reversal of the declining trends of productivity in the rural areas. The alleviation of the problem of growing mass poverty and the subsequent dynamization of internal demand forces also depend largely on the rapid improvement of rural incomes.[11]

Like the World Bank study, APPER was preoccupied with identifying and correcting the policy errors of the past and considered that good policies and good economic management were those that encouraged market forces. Thus, like the study, APPER focused on removing the constraints that make the economy uncompetitive and inefficient as well as on correcting structural defects, including price distortions, unrealistic exchange rates, trade imbalances, and disincentives to investment. Recovery was to be furthered by a system of supportive incentives ranging from better prices for agricultural products to extension services to improved infrastructure and marketing. Exports were to be supported by incentives, including the removal of bureaucratic constraints and easier access to foreign exchange. Like the Bank study and the structural adjustment programs, APPER advocated privatization, better cost recovery, more resource mobilization, and the curtailing of consumption.

In 1986 the United Nations prepared its own African recovery program, the United Nations Programme of Action for African Economic Recovery and Development, 1986-90 (UNPAAERD). It is not clear why the UN had its own program, since it was very similar to APPER. UNPAAERD placed the same emphasis on agriculture and the same emphasis on policy reform of the IMF kind. The program was based on mutual cooperation and revolved around two concerns: (a) the determination and commitment of the African countries to launch other national and regional programs of economic development; and (b) the response of the international community and its commitment to support and complement the African development efforts.[12] The estimated cost of the program was $57.4 billion, or 44.8 percent of the projected cost of APPER. The estimated cost of UNPAAERD was $128.1 billion, of which $82.46 billion was to be raised from domestic sources and $45.6 billion from external sources.[13]

Both APPER and UNPAAERD emphasized Africa's responsibility for its plight and for finding a solution. It is not difficult to understand why the leaders of the world community as well as African leaders emphasized this

11. OAU (1985).
12. United Nations (1986).
13. United Nations (1991, p. 63).

point. For Western leaders, who were increasingly irritated by Africans' blaming them for the effects of colonialism and imperialism, it vindicated not only their past relations to Africa but also their present perspective on African development. They could thus play down the structural deformities of African economies constituted under colonialism and gloss over the incorporation of Africa into the world capitalist system.

One reason why the Lagos plan was so resented was that it drew attention to these deformities, both their origins and their persistence. So it was highly significant that in APPER African leaders surrendered their position and became silent about those defects, blaming themselves for the continuation of underdevelopment. Apparently, the document prepared for the UN special session in 1986, popularly called *Africa's Submission*, was just that, a submission. The relish with which UNPAAERD has repeatedly drawn attention to Africa's culpability is palpable.

As far as African leaders were concerned, the emphasis on Africa's responsibility for its woes and the depiction of APPER as the embodiment of the Lagos plan was a face-saving device. But *Africa's Submission* was also born of a utilitarian calculation, to the effect that the West would be magnanimous to a humiliated African leadership ready and even eager to play the game the Western way.

Five years after the UN special session, UNECA carried out a survey to determine the extent to which African governments were implementing APPER and UNPAAERD. The survey showed that considerable effort was going into implementation. As regards investment in agriculture, 61 percent of the respondents said they had reached the target of 20–25 percent of total investment. The rate of compliance was higher in the area of macroeconomic management, in which 69 percent reported having embarked on structural adjustment programs and another 39 percent had undertaken stabilization measures. Among the macroeconomic reforms in place were exchange rate adjustment, public sector reduction, removal of subsidies, and freezing of wages. For example, 72 percent of the countries had embarked on the reduction of subsidies; 67 percent had initiated an employment freeze; 50 percent were carrying out exchange rate adjustments. As for the short- and medium-term measures for the support of agriculture, 67 percent were carrying out mechanization, 89 percent were engaged in the use of modern inputs, and 75 percent were developing agricultural research stations.

Unfortunately those who had set the agenda were not much interested in the question of compliance. The expected financial contribution from the industrialized countries did not come:

Nineteen months have now elapsed since the adoption by consensus of the Action program on July 1, 1986, and this is perhaps a sufficiently long enough time to monitor actions and assess the outcome of the joint efforts. A major success has been the resolve of Africans themselves to put their house in order, recognizing that primary responsibility for the development of their region rests first and foremost with them. This has amply been reflected in the actions taken at various national levels by the African governments. While African governments have showed the extent to which they are willing to go in order to get out of the economic crisis and in meeting the conditions that have been repeatedly emphasized by the major donors, it is regrettable that the efforts of the international community have not been up to expectations. Available statistics indicate that resource flows to Africa have declined further in real terms in 1987, and have been grossly inadequate to compensate for the fall in export earnings. This disappointing development in 1987, in terms of the response of the donor community, was reported by the Secretary-General of the United Nations in his first progress report in the 42nd Session of the General Assembly to assess the implementation of UNPAAERD, namely, that the African countries have done their utmost and have admirably honored their commitment so far, but that further deterioration in the external economic environment and the lack of adequate support from the international community have put the chances for the successful implementation of the program at serious risk.[14]

The UN secretary-general's 1991 report on UNPAAERD praised the African countries for their determination to tread the path of reform:

A majority of African countries have carried out policy reforms aimed at improving efficiency and the allocation of resources. These measures continued to be pursued, despite their often high political, social and economic costs, and have shown some positive results. By 1990, declines in economic output and in the delivery of social services had been slowed in many countries and even partially reversed in some. The ability to deploy additional resources effectively is stronger now than when the United Nations Program of Action began.[15]

Despite this effort, there was no chance that either APPER or UNPAAERD could take off, much less succeed, without the expected financial support

14. Adedeji (1988).
15. UNCTAD (1991, p. 10).

of the industrialized countries. In particular, an annual resource gap of $9.1 billion had to be filled if the program were to have any hope for success. Even if that money had been provided, the chances of success would still have been poor because of the $25 billion required annually for debt servicing. In the end the international support for UNPAAERD did not materialize, a point that the report dwells on repeatedly. For example, "Net resource flows to Africa, in real terms, actually declined from $25.0 billion in 1986 to $23.3 billion in 1990. Official development assistance (ODA) stagnated, in real terms, at around $16 billion annually during 1986–1989, while private flows fell sharply."[16]

Referring to the areas of trade and commodities, the report says that "in spite of the crucial importance of a favourable international economic environment to the success of African efforts towards recovery and development, little significant progress was registered. . . . Instead of reducing dependency on earnings from commodity exports, developments during the period of the *United Nations Programme of Action* reinforced the commodity-dependent trend of the 1980s, a decade that many think of as a period of stagnation and reversal for most African countries."[17]

Structural Adjustment and the Conflict of Agendas

One might think that the retreat of African leaders into APPER, UNPAAERD, and structural adjustment programs might have settled the controversy over the development agenda in Africa. But far from winding down, the controversy has been intensified. Africans have become increasingly frustrated with having to accept an exogenous agenda without even the compensation of a markedly improved performance or significant support from the metropolitan patrons that sponsored the agenda. This is painfully obvious in the case of UNPAAERD. African leaders are beginning to feel that there is little to be lost and much to be gained by adopting an African agenda. At the same time, African countries are more conscious of their weaknesses and the problems of resisting external pressure. Nonetheless, a declining confidence in the feasibility of the exogenous agendas, the worsening crisis, and Africa's increasing economic marginalization in the global system have all built momentum for an endogenous development agenda.

The contest over development agendas became especially intense and bitter with the introduction of structural adjustment programs. Structural

16. UNCTAD (1991, p. 8).
17. UNCTAD (1991, pp. 35, 36).

adjustment, based on the model of financial programming developed by Jacques J. Polak in 1957, is controversial, especially in regard to the relevance of its mix of theoretical assumptions to African conditions. Just how controversial it is among economists was highlighted by the Marshall lectures of 1987 given by Lance Taylor, an economist long associated with the World Bank. In insisting on austerity measures and the contraction of demands, the IMF maintains that the economy will not slacken but will simply reduce prices, especially those of nontraded goods; cut down the demand for imports; and expand exports to the benefit of the balance of payments. But Taylor showed that the IMF theory strings together a set of theoretical constructs—supply-determined output, substitution response, constant velocity, and the law of one price—any number of which may not be applicable in a particular historical context. If so, austerity measures will reduce output and bypass the reserve reallocation, hence reinforcing one of their major structural weaknesses. Apart from these theoretical problems, Africans fear that emphasis on market forces will perpetuate their location in the international division of labor in which they are relegated to the role of primary producers and mere consumers of manufactured goods.

In Nigeria, a political leadership torn between the fear of alienating the IMF and its patrons and the political repercussions of adjustment initiated a public debate over adjustment. Despite the government's effort to influence the debate, structural adjustment was overwhelmingly rejected. But the government went along with adjustment all the same. The economy had been so badly managed and was in such a poor state that the government feared that hostility from the Bretton Woods institutions and the West might lead to economic collapse and political chaos. The huge revenues from the oil boom had been so badly managed that after the peak of the boom in 1980 Nigeria went into continually increasing deficit. Its external debt, which had been no more than $4,284 million between 1960 and 1980, rose to $12,181 million in 1983. By 1986, when foreign exchange receipts had fallen to $6.8 billion from $26 billion in 1980, the external debt stood at an estimated $19.5 billion.[18] By 1985 there were grave doubts about Nigeria's creditworthiness, and it was becoming more difficult for Nigerian importers to open letters of credit. Imports dropped dramatically, from $15 billion in 1980 to $5.5 million in 1986. There were shortages of essential goods, manufacturing inputs, and spare parts. In June 1986 the government reluctantly embarked on a structural adjustment program.

18. Husain and Faruqee (1994, pp. 270-71).

It is at the pan-African rather than at the national level that the opposition of African leaders is most vocal. Their concern about structural adjustment, especially its social dimensions, has come out in many speeches at OAU ministerial and governmental meetings. The opposition to adjustment was most notably expressed in the pan-African meeting that produced *The Khartoum Declaration on the "Human Dimension of Africa's Economic Recovery and Development."* The meeting was held in Khartoum, Sudan, March 5–8, 1988, under the auspices of the United Nations as part of the follow-up to UNPAAERD and APPER and also as a sequel to the UNECA-sponsored international conference on Africa, The Challenge of Economic Recovery and Accelerated Development, held in Abuja, Nigeria, June 15–19, 1987, which produced the Abuja Declaration.

The Khartoum meeting, which brought together senior officials from African governments and UN agencies, including the IMF and the World Bank, showed that African opposition to structural adjustment had hardened. The declaration pointedly attacked the structural adjustment programs for aggravating the human condition in Africa, because they are "incomplete, mechanistic and of too short a time perspective." They are "incomplete because they are often implemented as if fiscal, trade and price balances are ends in themselves and are virtually complete sets of means to production increases. Human condition imbalances as related to employment, incomes, nutrition, health and education do not receive equal priority in attention to macro-economic imbalances." They are "mechanistic in being inadequately grounded in, or sensitive to, specific national economic, human and cultural realities. This is aggravated by an incomplete articulation which allows the gaps between macro models and contextual realities to remain largely unobserved." Finally, structural adjustment programs are effected "in too short a time perspective. Africa cannot wait for the attainment of external equilibrium and fiscal balances before seeking to improve the human condition nor can a long-term investment to strengthen the institutional, scientific, technical and productive capacity operating in environmental balance be postponed."[19]

Strangely, as the opposition to the Bretton Woods institutions' agenda spread in Africa and became more vehement, more African countries were adopting structural adjustment. They were worried about their deteriorating economies and feared that to invite the hostility of the West by rejecting structural adjustment might plunge their economies deeper into crisis. Thus while insisting that the IMF was "a mad doctor" to be avoided,

19. UNECA (1988, p. 21).

President Kaunda of Zambia was submitting to a structural adjustment package. At the same time the IMF and the Bank, forever confusing compliance with consent, were insisting on an emerging consensus on the need for structural adjustment in Africa. Meanwhile the debate over what to do about the crisis and about development in general was getting more strident in tone and more ideological in thrust, with the Bank and the Fund insisting that adjustment was the only way out and African leaders insisting with equal vigor that the only way out was to find an alternative to adjustment and the policies of the Bretton Woods institutions.

The problems and confusion of a situation in which African leaders are running their economies with a program they condemn have been compounded by the rift between the main UN agency responsible for economic development in Africa, UNECA, and the Bretton Woods institutions. After years of demurring politely, UNECA has now joined the African governments in criticizing structural adjustment programs; it is now the leader and the coordinator as well as the leading ideologue of this opposition. By joining the opposition, UNECA is undermining the scientific authority of the Bank and the IMF, an important part of their influence in Africa. UNECA's objections to structural adjustment, which, like those of other agencies such as UNICEF (United Nations Children's Fund), were usually restrained and polite, were sharpened when the agency felt that far from acknowledging the tragic problems of structural adjustment in Africa, the Bretton Woods institutions were deliberately distorting facts to buttress the legitimacy of the program.

The indictment largely stemmed from *Africa's Adjustment and Growth in the 1980s*, a publication that the World Bank had put out in 1989 to demonstrate the soundness of structural adjustment as a program of recovery. Its allegedly careless and insensitive attempt to justify the policy prescriptions of the Bretton Woods institutions appears to have deeply offended the African intelligentsia and policymakers. Having compared this World Bank report with their own practical experience and the midterm review of UNPAAERD, they felt that it was openly and crudely manipulative, and that it misrepresented the African crisis by focusing on disingenuous explanations and statistical analysis.

Subsequently, the twenty-fourth session of UNECA and the fifteenth meeting of the UNECA Conference of Ministers in Addis Ababa, April 6–10, 1989, passed a resolution expressing concern about this report. Not only was the report at variance with the midterm review of UNPAAERD and the consensus report of the forty-third session of the General Assembly on the same subject; it was even at variance with another study by the

World Bank: *Beyond Adjustment: Toward Sustainable Growth with Equity in Sub-Saharan Africa* (1988). The resolution called on the executive secretary of UNECA "to publish a paper highlighting the technical and statistical variances contained in the World Bank/UNDP report for an objective evaluation of the economic situation on the continent," and requested "that the ECA paper should be widely disseminated so as to put the record straight." The result was a new study by UNECA called *Statistics and Policies: ECA Preliminary Observations on the World Bank Report, "Africa's Adjustment and Growth in the 1980's."*

This study challenged the three major conclusions of the Bank-UNDP report:

that external conditions including export earnings and terms of trade and export prices were more favorable to Africa than usually assumed;

that internal conditions, including institutional weaknesses and structural rigidities, "have limited the ability to adjust from the exceptionally good years of the late 1970s and the early 1980s"; and

that the prospects for recovery are better than usually assumed. The UNECA analysis focused on the claim that structural adjustment was working as expected but that the performance of African economies improved with their commitment to adjustment reform.

Reviewing the evidence, UNECA argued that the Bank-UNDP report was manipulative in its use of statistics to confirm unfounded preconceptions and that it misrepresented the success of structural adjustment programs by failing to take account of the social costs of adjustment, its adverse long-term effects, its arbitrary classifications, and the distortions caused by the greater flow of external funds to adjusting countries. For its statistical calculations, the World Bank had used unweighted averages and 1985, an exceptionally good year, as its base year, whereas UNECA used weighted averages and 1980 as the base year.

UNECA argued that, contrary to the Bank's claims, the nonadjusting countries were outperforming the adjusting countries. According to UNECA, for the period 1980–87 "the performance of Sub-Saharan African countries with strong SAPs [structural adjustment programs] was the worst of any group; a negative annual average growth rate of 0.53 percent contrasted with a positive 2.0 percent for countries with weak structural adjustment programs and a relatively strong 3.5 percent for non-adjusting countries in sub-Saharan Africa."[20]

This was more than a debate about the implications of policy for growth

20. Morna (1989, p. 46).

rates. Part of the reason why this debate has become a public issue everywhere in Africa is the question of the social cost of adjustment, raised initially by such groups in Africa as trade unions and professional organizations like the Council for the Development of Economic and Social Research in Africa but, as mentioned, later taken up by international organizations like UNICEF and UNECA. UNECA, which was then led by Professor Adebayo Adedeji and was seen as being close to African aspirations, has been particularly sensitive to this issue. For instance, in its 1989 report it reiterated this concern: "There is mounting evidence that stabilization and structural adjustment programs are rending the fabric of the African society. Worse still, their severest impact is on the vulnerable groups in the society—children, women and the aged—who constitute two-thirds of the population."[21]

Steps have been taken to redress this problem by the Fund and the Bank, especially the latter, which now has a small unit on the Social Dimensions of Adjustment. But people outside the Bretton Woods institutions who are concerned with the social cost of adjustment worry that not enough is being done.

Opposition to the structural adjustment program eventually went beyond criticism to the search for an alternative program. The meeting of African finance ministers and other government officials that convened in Blantyre, Malawi, in March 1989 under the auspices of UNECA adopted an alternative program for economic recovery and development, published as *African Alternative Framework for Structural Adjustment Programs for Socio-Economic Recovery and Transformation.*

Alternative Framework is not simply a critique of the IMF-World Bank structural adjustment programs but potentially an alternative development agenda. Unlike the structural adjustment programs, it is dealing not merely with a crisis but with what it considers the root causes of underdevelopment in Africa. The report begins with an analysis of the colonial origins and structural deformities of African economies. It notes the arbitrary geography of the African countries, a veritable legacy of colonialism: 14 countries are landlocked, 23 countries have a population of fewer than 5 million, and 13 have a landmass of fewer than 50,000 hectares each. It shows how these and other factors have created a dependency syndrome, structural imbalance, and monocultural economies.[22]

The point is that the problems of Africa are not short term or ones that can be solved by monetarism but problems that need a comprehensive

21. UNECA (1989b).
22. UNECA (1989a).

agenda and a long-term perspective. The difference between the two agendas can be seen not only in these broader concerns but also in the extent to which *Alternative Framework* rejects the main policy measures of structural adjustment. Excessive budgetary reductions through the removal of subsidies, the curtailment of social programs, and so forth, are rejected for causing too much suffering and social strife and the depreciation of human resources to the detriment of future development.

The general emphasis of structural adjustment on drastic devaluation is decried for having too many negative effects, including inflation, the high cost of imported inputs, capital flight, and the entrenchment of traditional exports. Import liberalization is said to endanger endogenous industrialization and to perpetuate dependence. Relying on market forces tends to distort national priorities and to fuel inflation. By opposing these policy options, *Alternative Framework* underlines UNECA's distrust of the neoclassical assumptions of the development paradigm.

Important differences between the *Alternative Framework* agenda and the IMF-World Bank structural adjustment programs are evident not only in what the former rejects but also in the policy commitments it makes for strengthening and diversifying productive capacity in Africa, improving the level and distribution of income, satisfying basic human needs, and giving institutional support for adjustment with transformation. For instance, in its pattern of expenditure for the satisfaction of human needs, *Alternative Framework* suggests selective subsidies and price incentives to increase the supply of essential commodities to support welfare and create an enabling environment for development. It also suggests more government expenditure on the social sectors like health and education to improve human capital and to meet essential social needs. Thus it affirms the rationality of the welfarism that adjustment policies decry.

Whether these policies are feasible in the light of resource constraints is another matter. In the area of institutional support for adjustment with transformation, *Alternative Framework* suggests the institutionalization of the economic participation of previously marginalized groups such as artisans, peasants, and women and insists on popular involvement in decisionmaking to improve motivation, confidence in government, and the commitment of the people to the pursuit of collective goals. The Bretton Woods institutions, especially the World Bank, are also increasingly endorsing the need for participation, as is clear from the long-term perspective study *Sub-Saharan Africa: From Crisis to Sustainable Growth.*[23]

23. World Bank (1989b).

The differences between UNECA and the OAU on the one hand and the Bretton Woods institutions on the other are moving beyond policies and strategies and agendas and assuming an ideological form. Nowhere is this more evident than in the UNECA's attempt to locate its alternative agenda in a broader framework. In a speech on the African Crisis on October 25, 1990, the executive secretary of UNECA argued that *Alternative Framework* differs from the approach of the Bretton Woods institutions in four major ways. First, it is human centered. "It distances itself completely from the orthodox mechanistic models or approaches that have reduced the entire business of adjustment to the attainment of a few balances such as balance-of-payment equilibrium and reduced government budget deficits without any regard to the implications of the social sectors and the overall welfare of the people." Second, it is a holistic approach to socioeconomic change. That means it does not focus on a few selected economic variables but rather situates change in the broader context of social, political, cultural, and economic values and institutions. Third, its policies derive their "validity and legitimacy from the very structural nature of the African political economy." That means, for instance, that its policies "are based on a full grasp of the fact that the basic manifestations of the African structural distortions include elements like the predominance of subsistence and mere trading activities; narrow, urban bias of public policies; neglected informal sector; fragmented markets; etc." Fourth, it is sensitive to specificity. It "refrains from proposing a program to be applied in all countries at all times as has been the discernible tendency with the orthodox 'ready-made' programs of adjustment that have been proposed to Asian, Latin American and African countries alike."[24] These comparisons clearly strain beyond policy options to ideological leanings.

The contrast between the IMF-World Bank approach and UNECA's *Alternative Framework* exacerbates the confusion of development agendas. UNECA is nowhere near as powerful in Africa as the World Bank or the IMF, but it is influential. It has the prestige of the UN body charged specifically with the development of Africa. African policymakers think highly of its technical mastery of the economic issues of development. Although it is a UN organ, African leaders trust it and assume it is more attentive to African nationalist interests than other international organizations. Hence they have tended to use their UNECA ministerial meetings for building consensus and, more important, for developing common positions in their relations to external bodies, especially the IMF and the

24. Adedeji (1990).

World Bank. It is now very difficult to distinguish between the views of the community of African leaders and those of UNECA as an institution. Because of this special relationship, when UNECA puts out something like *Alternative Framework*, it is taken seriously in Africa.

The international development agencies I have discussed are not the only ones dealing with African development. There are many other development agencies whose influence on policy in Africa is far less than that of the World Bank, the IMF, and UNECA but nonetheless is quite significant in specific policy areas and in particular African countries. Some examples are the UNDP, the International Labor Organization, the Food and Agricultural Organization, the U.S. Agency for International Development, and the Swedish International Development Agency. These have their own agendas, too, which are not always mutually consistent. And within the same agencies agendas may shift with little consistency or continuity.

Indeed, there are shifts and discontinuities and some advance in the World Bank's 1980s and early 1990s blueprints for Africa.[25] For instance, the Bank has become more sensitive to the social impact of structural adjustment and to the need to invest in human resource development even while giving the market more scope. *Sub-Saharan Africa* shows that the Bank is now more sympathetic to regional integration and less apolitical; it now recognizes the significance of the governance factor. Still, the major thrust of the agenda of the Bretton Woods institutions is clear and largely predictable, and the problems arising from these shifts and discontinuities are not of the same magnitude as the differences between endogenous and exogenous development agendas and between what African leaders want to do and what they have to do.

The program outlined in UNECA's *Alternative Framework* does not appear to have emerged as a credible alternative policy. It has not been able to stem the tide of structural adjustment; if anything, the tide continues to rise. This may mean that the scientific status of the alternative framework is suspect, or it could be its sense of realism or the political will of its proponents that is suspect. Although a little convergence has occurred between the *Alternative Framework* program and the World Bank's structural adjustment programs, these two approaches nonetheless

25. The studies in chronological order are the following: *Accelerated Development in Sub-Saharan Africa: An Agenda for Action* (1981); *Sub-Saharan Africa: Progress Report on Debt Prospects and Programs* (1983); *Toward Sustained Development in Sub-Saharan Africa: A Joint Program of Action* (1984); *Financing Adjustment with Growth in Sub-Saharan Africa* (1986–90); *Africa's Adjustment and Growth in the 1980s* (1989); *Sub-Saharan Africa: From Crisis to Sustainable Growth* (1989); and *Adjustment in Africa: Reforms, Results and the Road Ahead* (1994).

still encode a rift between what African leaders want to do and what they have to do.

Conclusion

As suggested earlier, the problem in Africa is not so much that development has failed as that it never really got started. At the beginning of the independence period, African leaders, with few exceptions, were so absorbed in the struggle for power and survival and so politically isolated by their betrayal of the nationalist revolution that they could not launch a national development project but instead opted for dependent development, letting their metropolitan patrons determine the agenda and find the resources to implement it. Thus policymaking was largely divorced from political responsibility and development strategy was dissociated both from social needs and from the cultural and historical realities of the developing society. This dissociation led to development policies that have been more disruptive than developmental. Development could not proceed in a situation in which the national leadership had no vision or agenda of its own and relied on outsiders.

In due course African leaders found that their opportunistic resignation to dependent development was not as acceptable as they had imagined. Some of them began to evolve their own notions of how to proceed. But that did not help the takeoff of the development project, which was now hampered by the clash between the Africans and their metropolitan patrons and by a confusion of agendas, a confusion later compounded by the differences in the agendas of the multilateral development agencies, especially the Bretton Woods institutions and UNECA.

This confusion would not have mattered much if the leaders had been in a position to carry out their preferred agenda. But they were too economically dependent externally and too weak politically to challenge their economic dependence. So they were left with an uncomfortable dilemma. They could present their preferred program such as outlined in *The Lagos Plan of Action* or *Alternative Framework*, but lacking the resources and the will to soldier on in self-reliance, they could not do much with it. On the other hand, they could count on some assistance in implementing an exogenous agenda such as the agenda of *Accelerated Development* or structural adjustment, which was invariably not as sensitive to nationalist aspirations and not as politically risky as their own programs, since it came from people who could not be held responsible for their failures. Even as the opposition of African governments to the

IMF's structural adjustment programs spread and evolved into an alternative approach, more African countries continue to adopt and implement structural adjustment programs.

In this context, development becomes alienating on all sides. The outsiders that fashion the agenda are alienated from it the very moment it is created, because it is for others. Although it may be desirable for them to make the agenda stick as a manifestation of their values or power, they need not take serious interest in it, especially if such commitment entails significant costs. Thus after the UN General Assembly's special session on the African crisis and the concoction of UNPAAERD and APPER, their creators made little contribution toward their implementation. Considerable trouble has gone into establishing structural adjustment as the new orthodoxy, but except in a few countries such as Ghana, it has gotten so little support that even the Bretton Woods institutions have been critical of the neglect. Their plea for support is not likely to change much.

For the African leaders the alienation is more ominous. They are saddled with a strategy that hardly any of them believe in and that most of them condemn. They put up with it to avoid economic sanctions and in the hope of eliciting material support from external patrons. Invariably the support does not come, but, weak and fearful, they persist in hope. Lacking faith in what they are doing and caught between their own interests, the demands of their external patrons, and their constituents, African leaders tend to be ambivalent, confused, and prone to marginalize development and even their role in its pursuit. The development of Africa will not start in earnest until the struggle over development agendas is determined.

3

Improbable Strategies

I have been arguing that the problem in Africa is not so much that development failed as that it never really began. Nonetheless, elites in power in Africa have had to make an elaborate show of seeking development. In this chapter I examine what they have done in the name of development.

To begin with, one must be aware of the tendency to ignore history, which has been the bane of analyses of the development experience in Africa. Development strategies and policies do not simply emerge and get implemented, their feasibility and success being determined by their formal character. Strategies and policies are made and managed by a government in office and a political elite in power in a historical state and under a particular configuration of social forces. One cannot understand development policies and strategies, let alone the possibility of development, without referring constantly to the nature of the state and the dynamics of the social forces in which it is embedded.

Instead of being a public force, the state in Africa tends to be privatized, that is, appropriated to the service of private interests by the dominant faction of the elite. The society in which the African state exists is typically segmented into small rival political communities, often with strong localized identities, competing to capture and exploit state power or at least prevent it from oppressing them.

The nature of the state and the political context of development in Africa is such that, with minor exceptions, the commitment of most African leaders to development is at best ambiguous. Given a choice between social transformation, especially development, and political domination, most African leaders choose the latter. Because of circumstances that reach back to the colonial experience, most African states tend to be in hostile relation to the bulk of their population.

These are the underlying realities that have made the pursuit of development in Africa perfunctory, contradictory, and ineffective. Against this background I discuss what African governments have tried to do about development.

Agriculture

Somewhat surprisingly, the multilateral development agencies, especially the World Bank and donor countries, have been more interested in agricultural development than most African governments, which are usually focused on industrialization. The Bank's understanding of the significance of agriculture is evident in its many reports and policy papers and in its economic blueprints such as the long-term perspective study *Sub-Saharan Africa: From Crisis to Sustainable Growth* (1989). A 1993 study states:

> Achieving the economic growth objective for the region of at least 4 percent to 5 percent a year—as set forth in the Bank's long-term perspective study—requires agricultural growth rates of at least that amount. Agriculture still accounts for about a third of the region's GDP, and its role in economic transformation is crucial for its provision of investment capital, foreign exchange, and labor to other sectors of the economy. Agricultural production is also the most important source of the income needed to improve food security and reduce poverty, as most of the poor and food insecure are rural people.[1]

This understanding of the role of agriculture in development is manifested in the lending patterns of the Bank and the donor countries, as table 3-1 shows.

The Bank's understanding of the importance of agriculture has not, unfortunately, been matched by success in promoting agricultural production. For instance, on the Bank's own admission, at least 50 percent of its agricultural projects in Africa have failed, its highest failure rate in the world.[2] The underlying reasons for this failure are the same as the reasons why African governments have paid relatively limited attention to agriculture and have had poor policy performances: the marginalization of women, the refusal to take poor people and their interests seriously, the insufficient commitment to participative development, and the desire to control what the farmer produces and how.

1. World Bank (1993a, p. 109).
2. Callaghy and Ravenhill (1993, p. 22).

TABLE 3-1. *Lending to Borrowers in Africa, by Sector, Fiscal Years 1984–93*
Millions of U.S. dollars

Sector	Annual average, 1984–88	1989	1990	1991	1992	1993
Agriculture and rural development	509.6	754.8	997.4	504.9	697.5	318.3
Development finance companies	188.7	311.6	127.6	138.8	419.9	n.a.
Education	108.3	88.2	350.7	265.9	402.9	417.4
Energy, oil, gas, and coal	34.0	31.2	0.0	300.0	48.5	0.0
Power	130.1	138.4	230.0	155.0	76.0	356.0
Industry	89.5	81.4	105.1	n.a.	406.0	335.8
Nonproject	358.5	1,019.0	271.6	832.6	895.0	414.2
Population, health, and nutrition	65.6	81.3	232.7	432.8	100.3	131.2
Public sector management	51.3	0.0	45.6	5.7	76.7	20.6
Small-scale enterprises	17.4	270.0	130.0	0.0	0.0	0.0
Technical assistance	69.9	144.6	56.0	81.9	88.0	131.8
Telecommunications	29.4	103.3	225.0	12.8	n.a.	89.1
Transportation	382.4	248.7	543.6	309.5	242.8	474.5
Urban development	111.2	414.0	360.4	98.3	222.6	61.2
Water supply and sewerage	61.8	238.2	257.2	256.0	297.4	67.2
Total	2,207.7	3,924.7	3,932.9	3,394.2	3,973.6	2,817.3
World Bank	828.2	1,560.6	1,147.0	662.9	738.4	47.0
International Development Association	1,379.5	2,364.1	2,785.9	2,731.3	3,235.2	2,770.3
Number of operations	79	81	86	77	77	75

SOURCE: World Bank (1993a, p. 106). Numbers are rounded.

Agriculture is the area where policies touch the lives of the majority of people. In Africa 50 to 80 percent of the population lives in rural areas, and this rural population is predominantly peasant farmers. Agriculture accounts for about 40 percent of gross domestic product, 30 percent of exports, and 75 percent of employment.[3] Yet in 1978, after almost two decades of independence, agriculture in Sub-Saharan Africa received only 9 percent of government expenditure, less than the 10.5 percent given to defense.[4] As Jaycox rightly says, "If agriculture is in trouble, Africa is in trouble."[5]

The government's insufficient attention to agriculture as well as bad policies has impaired agricultural development and contributed to food dependence. The combination of relative indifference and poor policies caused food production per capita to fall by 0.1 percent a year in the 1960s and by 1.4 percent a year between 1970 and 1974. The World Bank reported in 1989 that in the previous thirty years agricultural exports declined steadily and food aid rose at 7 percent a year. But "despite the rapid growth in food imports, an average of about 100 million people in the early 1980s were undernourished—many more in years of poor harvest."[6]

It was not until the tragic food crisis of 1983–85 that the neglect of agriculture finally hit home. It was then agreed that investment in agriculture should be raised to between 20 and 25 percent of total public investment. Indeed, Africa's Priority Program for Economic Recovery (APPER), drawn up under the auspices of the Organization of African Unity (OAU), had proposed a total agricultural investment of $57.4 billion, or 44.8 percent of total investment.[7]

In considering agricultural development in Africa, it is useful to distinguish between the latent and the manifest functions of agricultural policies. More often than not, the former undermines the latter. The manifest function of policy demands an increase in agricultural productivity, but the latent function emphasizes control. And that is the turn that policy has taken in most of Africa: an obsessive concern with the control of what the peasant produces, how he or she produces it, and how the product is disposed of. Such are the underlying preoccupations that have distorted the concerns of most African governments with land reform; for example, the Land Use Decree in Nigeria (1978); settlement schemes,

3. Jaycox (1992, p. 29).
4. World Bank (1981).
5. Jaycox (1992).
6. World Bank (1989b).
7. OAU (1985).

such as the million-acre settlement scheme in Kenya; extension services, such as the World Bank agricultural development projects; and marketing through government-owned marketing boards.

The dialectics of development and control is well illustrated by the Sudanese irrigation scheme of Wad al Abbas. This scheme seems well intentioned, an attempt to increase the productivity of cotton farmers by providing irrigation, tractors, advisory services, pesticides, transport facilities, grading, ginning, and marketing. But this largesse effectively turned farmers into wage laborers:

> The scheme did not separate farmers from all means of production; however, it introduced insecurity of tenure. Farmers can lose their land if deemed negligent in cotton production. Between 1980 and 1982 alone at least a dozen Wad al Abbas farmers lost land this way. Farmers' ownership of means of production was further weakened by the intro-duction of pumps and other technology which is controlled by manage-ment. Ownership of a parcel of land on the scheme is meaningless without control over the technology required in production. For exam-ple, farmers have no control over the operation or maintenance of irrigation machinery. Insufficient irrigation is one of the main reasons they cite for poor yields.
>
> Control over the production process: with the establishment of the scheme, control over the production process was transferred from farmers to managers and policy-makers. The household remains the basic unit of production in that each household determines and orga-nizes its own labour inputs and contracts independently with any hired labourers or sharecroppers it employs. Each household also controls production on the sorghum plot. But farmers have no choice in the decision to grow cotton. And, all inputs to cotton beyond labour are determined by management. Farmers cannot limit inputs such as fertili-zer and aerial pesticide spraying or the prices at which they are supplied although they bear much of the cost. Farmers are also locked into a schedule as they receive water in succession along canal lines. Each must perform operations on time. Some observers of the Gezira Scheme have likened it to an assembly line.[8]

As that situation suggests, the approach of the Wad al Abbas project was more oriented to improved supply through irrigation, pest controls

8. Bernal (1988, p. 95).

and other measures than to distributional concerns like land tenure and pricing. This bias reflects, in turn, the divergence of interest between political elites and peasants.

The situation in Burundi also illustrates the tendency of African governments to control agricultural production. Until the early 1990s agricultural production and pricing were determined by administrative fiat. The government determined not only prices but also inputs, which it easily controlled by supplying free or at subsidized prices. The system of controls was exercised by government ministries and parastatals. Now the Cotton Management Company remains the sole vendor of cotton, and the Cotton Textile Company of Burundi is virtually the monopoly purchaser of cotton, buying 90 percent of the cotton sold by the Cotton Management Company. Coffee is similarly controlled by the Coffee parastatal, the Burundi Office of Industrial Cultures, which became the Office du Café in 1991.[9]

The latent function of agricultural policy, which expresses the interest of the political elites, can prevail over the manifest function because of highly asymmetrical relations of power between the elites and the peasantry. Political parties and political formations and interest groups representing the interests of peasants are rare in Africa. Rarer still are political formations with a peasant base strong enough to threaten the political elites or even muster sufficient resources to place the interests of the peasantry on the national agenda.

Political leaders with strong commitments to the interests of peasants have as a rule been brutally repressed, especially when they have tried to form political movements. A case in point was the murder in Kenya of J. M. Kariuki, who had been private secretary to President Jomo Kenyatta. Kariuki was so revolted by the way that the elites, including the president, were accumulating land amid acute land scarcity that he spoke out and incurred the wrath of the Kenyatta government.

Political parties or social movements with a peasant base have not been allowed to function. In Kenya, a splinter faction of the ruling Kenyan African National Union, which opposed the privatization of land, was systematically persecuted, and when it joined the opposition Kenya People's Union, that party was persecuted until it ceased to exist. In Ghana, Kwame Nkrumah's ruling Convention People's Party severely repressed the National Liberation Movement, which was affiliated with cocoa farmers, when the NLM opposed the government's cocoa-pricing policy. After constant persecution, including assassinations, the NLM was proscribed.

9. Husain and Faruqee (1994, p. 40).

...now for a more detailed look at agricultural development in two countries, Nigeria and Tanzania.

Agricultural Policy Initiatives in Nigeria

At independence, Nigeria, like most African countries, followed the line of least resistance and largely continued colonial economic policies. In agriculture this meant the promotion of selected export crops such as cocoa, groundnuts, and palm produce. The First National Development Plan, 1962-68, had no discernible agricultural strategy. No serious attempt was made to encourage private investment in agriculture; public investment was minimal and biased toward the interests of the elites. Of the total capital expenditure of N676.5 million for the plan period, 91.9 million, or 13.5 percent, was to go to primary production, including agriculture. Of this allocation, approximately 30 percent, the largest share, was for government-sponsored large-scale projects, especially plantations, irrigation schemes, and farm settlements; 23 percent for extension services; 13.3 percent for agricultural credit; 11 percent for research; 2.9 percent for research and training; 7 percent for processing and distribution; and 14.7 percent for unclassified projects. The allocation to agriculture, inordinately small to begin with, was largely unspent. In fact, 42.8 percent of the budgeted capital expenditure for the plan period was unspent. The government blamed this result on "the weakness of the Ministry of Agriculture especially in effective planning and coordination."

The plan and its pattern of expenditure were biased in favor of export crops. Food crops did not elicit much attention. This is perhaps understandable, since export crops, especially cocoa, groundnuts, cotton, rubber, and palm products, constituted 75 percent of Nigeria's export earnings. Also, food prices had been quite stable and food imports modest, about 10 percent of food requirements.

The decade of the oil boom, 1970-80, reinforced the neglect of agriculture. Because of the boom, export earnings increased from 1,000 million nairas in 1971 to N13,000 million in 1980. Much of the increase was due to the expansion of petroleum production and the rising price of petroleum. The period from 1973 to 1978 was the quintessential boom period. In 1974-75 revenue from petroleum increased by a multiple of five, and petroleum became Nigeria's main revenue base, accounting for 90 percent of exports. The boom led to a steep increase in federal expenditure, which doubled between 1973 and 1974 and again between 1974 and 1975.[10]

With the oil boom the significance of agriculture was reduced. Agriculture, which accounted for 75.9 percent of total federal revenue in 1965, was contributing only 2.4 percent by 1980; in contrast, petroleum's share rose from 2.7 percent in 1960, to 73.7 percent in 1971, to 96.1 percent in 1980. The oil boom and the rise in public expenditure that accompanied it had a negative impact on agriculture. The extraordinary rise in federal expenditure altered relative prices and wages markedly. As the World Bank study edited by Ishrat Husain and Rashid Faruqee correctly noted, "High wage and price increases secured the resources needed to accommodate the demand in nontraded goods, but they depressed the non-oil traded goods sectors. An exchange rate polity that allowed the naira to appreciate with rising oil revenues in combination with rising domestic costs meant a sharp detoriation in international competitiveness. The negative impact of these policies on agriculture was particularly severe."[11] For instance, by the second half of the 1970s the export of palm oil, cotton, and groundnuts, which had been the major foreign-exchange earners before the oil boom, had ceased. The demise of agriculture, especially staple crop production, and the reduction of the rural labor force by the civil war and urban migration (stimulated by the oil boom) put great pressure on the food supply and food prices.

In the Second National Development Plan, 1970–74, agriculture fared no better. This plan was preoccupied with postwar reconstruction. Allocation to the economic sector as a proportion of total expenditure declined. The chapter of the plan that reviewed policy measures did not discuss agriculture. The plan talked generally about ensuring adequate food supplies and expanding exports as well as about producing agricultural materials for extensive domestic manufacturing activities. But there was little by way of an action program or financial commitment. There were to be special agricultural development schemes, for which N3 million was provided, and a National Agricultural Credit Institution, which was to get N6 million. Federal grants to all the states for seed multiplication, extension services, fertilizers, pesticides and herbicides, irrigation equipment, tractors and other implements, storage facilities, publicity and information, feeds, and so forth, got all of N17 million.

The Third National Development Plan, 1975–80, reordered priorities between the productive sector and infrastructure development in favor

10. Husain and Faruqee (1994, pp. 240–41).
11. Husain and Faruqee (1994, p. 240).

of the former, which along with commerce got about 60 percent of estimated public investment. One would expect this to mean much more investment in agricultural development. But that was not the case. The plan appeared to have incorporated the views of the Consortium for the Study of Nigerian Rural Development, which did not give priority to agricultural investment, despite the background of the Sahelian drought (1972–74), declining food production, rising food prices, and escalating food imports. For instance, rice importation increased sevenfold in just one year, 1975 to 1976. Despite the impending food crisis, allocation to agriculture was only 5 percent of total expenditure. Policy favored capital-intensive, large-scale projects, particularly irrigation under the auspices of the River Basin Development Authorities (RBDAs).

The RBDAs were a major feature of agricultural policy in this plan period. There were to be three RBDAs initially. Each of the projects was expected to irrigate twenty to twenty-five hectares at a cost of between N135 million and N330 million. But there were considerable cost overruns; the total cost of the RBDAs was close to N2.5 billion.[12] Nobody now pretends that the RBDAs are cost effective or that they can ever be. Even if the initial capital outlay is written off, it is unlikely that returns can meet current costs alone. Most important, the RBDAs cannot meet the objective of producing enough to substitute for imported food, particularly wheat. And they have run into serious and continuing resistance from landowners and farmers, leading to violent conflicts and loss of lives.

Other major policy instruments for increasing food crops were the national accelerated food production program (NAFPP) and the integrated rural development projects. According to the third development plan, the NAFPP intended to make selected farmers produce improved seedlings of maize, rice, wheat, and cassava that could be distributed to other farmers. These selected farmers would effectively be running seed multiplication and demonstration plots. The schemes were poorly funded. The first progress report on the plan disclosed that only N1.167 million was made available to all the state governments of the federation to carry out this scheme. With such a level of funding the scheme could be only a gesture.

A more serious effort to boost agriculture, particularly food crop development, was the establishment of agricultural development projects (ADPs), initially launched in 1975 with pilot programs in Fatua (Katsina), Gusau (Sokoto), and Gombe (Bauchi). The programs were to be gradually

12. Beckman (1987, p. 114).

expanded to every state in Nigeria. Although they are joint ventures of the government and the World Bank, the ADPs are largely independent of the State Ministries of Agriculture and are managed by the World Bank.

The ADPs are less ambitious than the RBDAs, are less capital intensive, and are aimed not at the commercial farmer but at the smallholder. The ADPs exist to provide services and facilities to help the smallholder become more productive; for example, fertilizers, water supply, equipment, herbicides, pesticides, planning, and land-clearing infrastructure development. The projects, which cost $30 million each, are mainly funded (about 60 percent) by World Bank loans. According to the Bank's *Agricultural Sector Review* of 1979, the ADPs expect to reach into the rural areas and to "the productive reserve of 90 per cent of Nigeria's farming population."[13]

Despite the Bank's claims, there are many who doubt the cost-effectiveness of the ADPs and their contribution to agricultural development in Nigeria, issues to which I return shortly. Nevertheless, the ADPs constitute one of the few serious initiatives on agricultural development on the agenda and were far more useful to Nigerian agriculture than the large irrigation projects of the RBDAs. All the same, the Nigerian government continued to pour money into the large irrigation projects, while underfunding the ADPs. For example, the large-scale irrigation projects got 72.7 percent of total agricultural expenditure in 1980 and 76.2 percent in 1981, whereas the ADPs got only 4.1 percent in 1980 and 8.1 percent in 1981.[14]

By 1979 the problems of agricultural policy in Nigeria could be seen more clearly, and the government was greatly worried, particularly by the impending food crisis. The demand for food was growing at 3.5 percent a year, while the production growth rate was 1 percent a year. The government was projecting a deficit of 5.5 million tons of grain for the plan period 1981–85. Consequently, it became more sensitive to the deficiencies of its policy, a fact aptly reflected in the *Outline of the Fourth National Development Plan, 1981–85*.[15] For one thing, the governnment recognized that in the past there had hardly been an agricultural strategy, even a bad one. Although the outline claimed to have taken a comprehensive view of the problems of development in agriculture, such an approach did not emerge. But at least the need for such an approach had been recognized.

The outline was critical of the tendency in the past, especially in the

13. Beckman (1987, p. 113).
14. Sano (1983, p. 39).
15. Government of Nigeria (1981).

third plan, to emphasize capital-intensive large-scale projects such as the irrigation schemes. Because of the failure of those schemes and the increasing influence of the World Bank, the government declared it was shifting emphasis from large-scale farms, a focus that contributed very little to productivity, to smallholders, who account for 90 percent of the domestic food supply. The government also committed itself to expanding the ADPs, which it found to "have proved quite successful resulting in substantial improvements in incomes and living standards of the smallholder farmers in the project areas." But aware that the expansion of the ADPs would take a long time, the government devised a concurrent smallholder program, the accelerated development area program, for areas not yet covered by the ADPs. The program was to apply the core elements of the ADP approach, such as the supply of essential inputs to smallholders. This approach typified the ascendancy of the World Bank in the management of Nigerian agriculture.

Even so, Nigerian policymakers were ambiguous about their new commitment to a smallholder strategy. Curiously, the government continued to hang on to the big irrigation projects, which by its own admission were unproductive. Under the fourth plan, N34.432 million, or 4.1 percent of the government's agricultural expenditure, was allocated to the ADPs; irrigation projects got N613.161 million, or 72.7 percent of the expenditure. In 1981 the ADPs got N75.098 million, or 8.1 percent of agricultural allocations; the irrigation projects got N710.516, or 76.2 percent. How could the irrigation projects continue to be funded on this scale by a government that had found them incapable of achieving their objectives? Perhaps the Nigerian leaders were fond of grand projects. Also, so much money had already gone into the projects that it might have seemed less embarrassing to keep the RBDAs going than to abort them and fail conspicuously. Finally, for some highly placed people, the RBDAs and their irrigation projects provided excellent opportunities for easy wealth.

The most recent initiative in the area of agricultural development policy was yet another grand and costly project: the Directorate of Food, Roads, and Rural Infrastructure (DFRRI). Its function was to promote the development of agriculture and rural Nigeria by improving rural infrastructure, such as roads, water supply, electricity, and transportation; and to encourage the production of food by ensuring the availability and use of improved inputs, better implements, extension services, and so forth. The scale of the operation of the DFRRI can be gauged by its share of public expenditure, which dwarfs the allocation of every ministry and parastatal except one. The DFRRI got a budgetary allocation of N400 million in 1987 and

N500 million in 1988. In contrast, the Ministry of Education got N4 million in 1987 and N302 million in 1988; Health had N166.9 million in 1987 and N259.9 million in 1988; Industries, N191.2 million in 1987 and N260.2 million in 1988; Petroleum and Energy, N104.3 million in 1987 and N402 million in 1988. Only the Defense Ministry did better than the DFRRI, with N717.6 million in 1987 and N830 million in 1988.

The DFRRI was expected to function on the basis of social participation; that is, the government would provide financing or seed money for projects executed in cooperation with local communities. Instead it became the dispenser of huge lucrative contracts. The Nigerian press concurred that the DFRRI's presence in rural communities was difficult to see, that it existed largely on paper, and that it appeared to have served patronage and corruption more than agricultural development. Government-appointed inspectors found that the DFRRI made false claims about its accomplishments. Not surprisingly it has now been abolished.

The DFRRI illustrates the contradictions between the latent and manifest functions of public policy in Nigeria. The concept of the DFRRI is basically sound, in the double sense that the development of rural infrastructure, especially roads, is essential for expanding agricultural production and that it is desirable to effect this development by participative strategies. However, this essentially sound policy was subverted by a greedy and corrupt political class that set out to appropriate the huge resources of the DFRRI.

Nigerian Agriculture in the Era of Structural Adjustment

By 1976 public expenditure had expanded so much that Nigeria began to have a budget deficit; wages continued to rise, and the Nigerian naira appreciated rapidly, as much as 100 percent between 1973 and 1978. Nigeria became more and indebted. Despite a second oil boom between 1979 and 1982, the economy slid into crisis. By 1983 the budget deficit had grown to 12 percent of GDP, and real incomes, which had increased by 200 percent between 1972 and 1980, fell by 60 percent. Even as the terms of trade deteriorated and interest rates rose, the naira continued to appreciate in real terms, ensuring strong demand for foreign exchange and imports. The Economic Stabilization Act of 1982, which introduced a set of austerity measures including import restrictions and higher import duties, failed to alleviate the economic crisis. Growth rates, real incomes, and consumption fell steeply, as did the terms of trade. In July 1986 Nigeria was obliged to launch a structural adjustment program.

The problem is that under structural adjustment programs agriculture still remains a "residual" category, expected to derive residual benefits from deregulation rather than from more active programs encouraging agricultural production. Agricultural policy still suffers from class bias, which often translates into ill-conceived policies and contradictions between manifest and latent functions.

In Nigeria agricultural policy under structural adjustment has largely taken the form of deregulation, especially the abolition of monopoly commodity boards. The government did not launch any bold new initiatives for agricultural development, but it hoped that agriculture would benefit from the development of the infrastructure, especially roads, in the rural areas. The sign of government presence in agriculture lies somewhat incongruously in the occasional ADP office; in the odd local government area demonstration farms, where fertilizers may be obtained with a great deal of effort and some luck; and earlier in the DFRRI's sporadic efforts to improve the rural infrastructure.

The Nigerian experience in agricultural development is not typical; agriculture does not suffer because the political elite, interested in controlling agricultural surplus, confuses that concern with development policy. In Nigeria the enormous revenues from petroleum production make the control of agricultural surplus, as well as interest in agricultural development, unnecessary. Indeed, agriculture was so neglected that food imports became a major element of the Nigerian fiscal crisis. In 1961 oil contributed only 2.7 percent of total export earnings, while non-oil exports accounted for 97.3 percent. But the share of oil rose to 92.6 percent in 1975, and 96.1 percent in 1980, and the share of non-oil exports fell to 7.4 percent in 1975 and to 3.9 percent in 1980. The non-oil exports were predominantly primary commodities: groundnuts and groundnut oil, rubber, palm oil and palm kernel, cocoa, and cotton. The five export commodities had been reduced to three by 1974, when only rubber, palm oil and palm kernel, and cocoa were being exported. By 1980 two more export commodities had vanished, and only cocoa was being exported.

The Nigerian experience suggests that the problem is not so much failed policies but no policies and some self-serving measures. But despite the self-serving measures, the absence of policies, and the residual status of agriculture, there were some openings for agricultural development. For instance, even though the DFRRI became a means of corrupt appropriation for the elite in power, it did provide some infrastructure that improved farmers' facilities, especially roads and markets. The devaluation of the naira in 1992 made the internal terms of trade more favorable to rural people.[16] Agriculture also benefited from liberalization, especially of price and marketing controls. Indeed, the World Bank insists that agriculture benefited considerably from Nigeria's adjustment program.

What the gains of agriculture really tell us is not so much the success of present policies but the immense potential for improvements in the event of better policies. A 1994 Bank publication makes this point implicitly, illustrating the self-serving measures that often pass as public policies in Nigeria:

Agriculture. The allocation in the 1992 budget for fertilizer, the largest item in the capital allocation for the Ministry of Agriculture, is N0.6 billion, but the actual total procurement cost is estimated at N3.4 billion, and extra budgetary allocations will be required. Of the eleven ongoing large-scale irrigation projects, for which N181 million has been allocated, only three, representing N63 million of the allocation, are deemed viable. Public grain storage facilities, a component of the Federal Strategic Grain Reserve Program costing N1.6 billion, are not fulfilling the goal of stabilizing food prices and enhancing the food security of the poor. Under capital supplementation N150 million has been set aside for project execution by a newly established agency, the National Agricultural Land Development Authority (NALDA), whose mandate is to address the chronic problem of underutilized farm land and rural labour and the high cost of land development. This mandate duplicates the activities of other agencies.[17]

Agricultural Transformation in Tanzania

At independence in 1961, Tanzania, like Nigeria, did not initially try to change the inherited system of colonial agriculture. In particular, the country retained the colonial emphasis on export crops and may even have amplified it, since the variety of available food crops got smaller. Tanzania, however, managed the existing agricultural system with less efficiency than in the colonial era, if the rising food imports and declining exports are any guide. A Tanzanian scholar, L. A. Msambichaka, complains that "both during the colonial era and after independence, no state policy was seriously geared towards food self-sufficiency or improvement of the

16. World Bank (1994b, p. 147).
17. Husain and Faruqee (1994, p. 250).

human environment. Efforts have never been made to ensure that the nation is adequately supplied with enough food domestically."[18]

But this situation was more true of the first years of independence. Tanzania is distinguished for being one of the few African countries that initiated a program of rural and agricultural transformation. The transformation was pursued progressively through the village settlement scheme of 1964, the Ujamaa village program of 1967, and the villagization scheme of 1973.

A World Bank mission that visited Tanzania just before independence argued that (a) the prospects of agricultural development in Tanzania through the improvement of existing farming systems were poor, and (b) the more promising option would be through a very intense effort to transform agriculture through resettlement in new areas. In 1963 the newly independent government in Tanzania accepted the Bank analysis as the basis of its agricultural policy, and a Village Settlement Agency was duly established.

The idea of resettlement, which the British rulers of Tanzania had also supported, seemed reasonable in the country's circumstances. The settlement pattern of Tanzania's rural population was too scattered. As much as 94 percent of the country's rural population of 11 million lived in relatively isolated homesteads rather than villages. There was a compelling reason to develop agriculture because the country was dependent on agriculture. Yet agriculture was still largely subsistence farming (59 percent of agriculture at independence).[19] It was difficult to give the necessary support to peasant producers when the limitation of resources was greatly compounded by the scattered pattern of settlement. For instance, Tanzania had only 373 doctors in 1967, a ratio of 1 doctor to 31,842 people.[20] It is therefore not surprising that Tanzania embarked on resettlement.

The early settlement schemes were largely voluntary. The settlers came mainly from such regions of land scarcity as Kilimanjaro. The settlers were liberally provided with inputs, services, and farm machinery. However, this benign approach to settlement was marred by paternalism and meddlesome officialdom. Even the liberal supply of equipment and services became a problem. It was disruptive and in some instances it encouraged the attitude that machines will do the work. But most important, the oversupply of tractors and other farm technology—in Upper Kiteli a farm

18. Mkandawire (1987, p. 124).
19. McHenry (1979, p. 3).
20. McHenry (1979, p. 3).

of 1,600 acres run by 100 families was given 10 tractors—saddled the settlers with debts they could not repay.[21]

The concept of agricultural development through resettlement schemes was to change as a result not only of the failure of these earlier schemes but also of Tanzania's flirtation with socialism in the wake of the Arusha Declaration of 1967. A central concept of this socialism was Ujamaa, which means family head. Ujamaa, whose components are mutual respect, common property, and communal labor, also became Tanzania's strategy of agricultural development. The ruling party, Tanzania African National Union (TANU), began to encourage people to form Ujamaa villages. Official policy was still committed to voluntary settlement, but government and party officials, anxious to look like pioneers of progress, became increasingly manipulative and coercive to achieve a higher rate of resettlement in the communal villages. For all that, there were no more than 800 Ujamaa villages by 1969.

Dissatisfied by the slow growth of Ujamaa villages, the party and the presidency increased the pressures for their formation. President Julius Nyerere launched the plan to move everyone in the Dodoma area to Ujamaa villages and, to emphasize the importance of resettlement, lived in one settlement village, Chamwino, for some time. Government and party officials then became militant about moving people to villages. Since the movement tended to be hostile to commercial farming, it stirred up strong antipathies and even led to clashes and the assassination of a senior party official, Wilbert Klerruu. According to government statistics, the number of Ujamaa villages rose from 1,956 in 1970 to 5,556 in 1972.[22] But these statistics should be treated cautiously. Government and party officials had become so zealous about creating Ujamaa villages that they registered as Ujamaa, villages that had no communal farming activities. Some were merely existing villages into which people from surrounding homesteads were crowded.

This enthusiasm was carried to a point where some officials talked about villagization as waging war, thus underlining the political elites' self-absorbed construction of values. Despite its apparent radicalism, suggested by its commitment to the abolition of commercial farms, the autonomy of the villages, and the empowerment of peasants, Ujamaa moved on inexorably to enhancing the role of party and government officials. These officials, anxious to show results to please TANU and protect their

21. Hyden (1980, p. 72).
22. Hyden (1980, p. 103).

careers and privileges, were impatient with democratic procedures and became increasingly authoritarian.

Ujamaa villages had actually been planned to have their own local government; hence they were not subject to the jurisdiction of the national Ward Development Committee (WDC) and the TANU branch. They had their own Ward Development Committees and their own TANU branch. But studies of the Ujamaa in the West Lake Region show that the intended localization of democracy was not realized. The decisionmaking organs were the WDC and the General Meeting. The General Meeting, an assembly of all adults in the village and all government and party staff, was supposed to be the sovereign body of the Ujamaa village. But it usually met only once a year. Apart from electing the WDC, the General Meeting became largely ceremonial. And the democratic possibilities of the WDC were dissipated by informality, infrequent meetings, meetings with unclear official status, selective invitations, and the making of decisions outside official channels. This situation allowed party and government officials to exercise real power, particularly the agricultural field officer (AFO), who was responsible to the government for the operation of the village and who by virtue of that role was also responsible for all communication between the village and the government.

The zeal of officials to show results may have undermined their sense of realism. For instance, the four-year plan of Ntobeye projected banana cultivation of eighty hectares, bore hole, fishpond, a large herd of goats, dairy cows, beef cattle. They would require a total investment of TSh1,289,000 for a cattle dip, stoves, maize grinders and shellers, 80 draft oxen, water supply, bulldozer, two tractors, and so on.[23] By the standards of what was possible, as reflected in the already considerable experience of villagization in Tanzania, this was more a fantasy than a plan. The lack of realism on the part of officials and their effort to bring performance toward their plan targets made them coercive and increased the alienation of officials and peasants to the detriment of productivity. It is not surprising that for all its good intentions Ujamaa did not bring about the expected increase in productivity.[24]

The response of the Tanzanian government and TANU to the problems of agricultural development through Ujamaa was, interestingly enough, more paternalism and coercion, this time tainted with barely repressed anger. Officials felt that the people had let them down by not taking

23. Bosen (1977).
24. Hyden (1980, pp. 110–12); Awiti (1973); Mohele (1975).

more enthusiastically to the Ujamaa movement and not working harder to produce more.

On November 6, 1973, President Nyerere announced a new policy of compulsory villagization. In an uncharacteristically angry speech, the president reprimanded Tanzanians for not reciprocating all the effort and sacrifices the leadership had made to serve their needs and for frustrating the country's socialist development policies through indifference and idleness. The president said that, although he could not compel Tanzanians to be socialists, he would ensure that all Tanzanians lived in Ujamaa villages by 1976. As many as 5 to 6 million people may have moved in what was a gigantic operation of unprecedented mass movement of people in Africa. Everything was pressed into the service of the operation—TANU cadres, the media, the army, the police, and the civil service. The government mounted a massive propaganda effort to promote the move, portraying people who opposed moving as individualist, selfish, antisocial, unpatriotic, and even immoral.

Convinced that one reason for the program's lack of success was the attitudes and activities of "petit-bourgeois elements," the government announced the removal of all middlemen in commerce and trade. Under Operation Maduka, private shops were closed and replaced with cooperatives; goods were to be distributed directly by officials or by Ujamaa shops. These measures were predictably disastrous, since they threw the distribution system into confusion, and quickly led to the disappearance of essential commodities like kerosene, sugar, and soap. Sensing popular discontent, the government restored licenses to some private stores and agreed that private stores could operate until viable Ujamaa stores were available. Operation Maduka slowed down but continued to advance. By 1977 the number of Ujamaa and cooperative dukas (shops) was 3,284, about 11 percent of the number of private dukas.[25]

It is paradoxical that while using coercion to move millions of people, often against their will, to new homes and new relations of production and new life-styles, the leadership of Tanzania continued to phrase its goals in emancipatory values, in terms of the empowerment of the people by improving their productivity and providing better amenities for them; in essence, freeing the people from the exploitative grip of the petite bourgeoisie. The paradox comes into clearer relief when political reforms that accompanied compulsory villagization are examined.

25. Hyden (1980, p. 132).

The political reforms, like the economic ones, were presented as ways to institutionalize effective local government and facilitate the participation of the grass roots in government and to destroy the power of "local notables," who had used the District Councils (whose power was not drastically diminished) to manipulate and control the rural population. Instead, what the political reforms did was to facilitate government control of the rural population and its productive activities. Under the reforms, the regions received the status of ministries, with the regional party secretary as the political head and a newly created post, the development director (which was analogous to the principal secretary of a ministry), in charge of development, clearly the main business of government and society.

The structural and functional differentiation within the bureaucracy that existed at the level of the central government was done away with. All the responsibilities that would normally be handled by different ministries were now fused in one monolithic structure and in one person, the regional party secretary. Aided by a technocratic arm, the development director, he or she made every major decision about every sphere of social and economic life, and he or she was the link between the region and the central government and the party. The regional party secretary controlled all development activities—this control was the very inspiration for these political reforms. This system has actually rolled back the development of civil society because it has drastically reduced the prospect of autonomous development initiatives.

The same regional structure was replicated with the same effect at the level of the village. By 1977 the government decided to post officials to each village, called village managers. Although they were to function under the Village Council, their status as the central government in the village tended to place the Village Council effectively under them, especially since they were also the designated managers of the productive activities of the village. Here again control overrode development and even party ideology.

To conclude, in a certain sense the pursuit of agricultural development through Ujamaa was a modest success: the policy certainly succeeded in its objective of consolidating residential patterns in rural Tanzania. The Tanzania government claimed that within a decade of villagization, 13,500,000 peasants were consolidated into 7,300 villages, a fact that reflects 90 percent compliance of the rural population.[26] President Nyerere

26. *Daily News* (Dar es Salaam), December 28, 1977, p. 1.

may well have been correct in insisting that this consolidation laid the foundation for a better life for the people of Tanzania. However, the problems and failures of the policy were immense.[27]

The people did not accept the TANU notion of communalism, and though they generally lived in Ujamaa villages, they rejected its communal demands, a posture demonstrating that the content was lost to the form. After a decade of villagization, less than 2.5 percent of GDP was derived from communal agricultural activity.[28] The Ujamaa movement did not transform Tanzanian agriculture and did not succeed in its ambitious plans of increasing productivity.

These failures were the result of putting control by the political class ahead of development. All the major contradictions of the Ujamaa movement arose from paternalism, coercion, and the self-centered presumptions of the political class.

Tanzanian Agriculture under Structural Adjustment

In its first six years of independence, 1961–67, Tanzania achieved a laudable growth rate of 6 percent a year; between 1967 and 1973 its GDP was still growing at nearly 5 percent a year. But external shocks, such as the steep rise of oil prices, drought, and poor policies, began to take their toll; growth declined and indebtedness increased. The agricultural growth rate declined to 2 percent a year. Between 1976 and 1985 agricultural exports fell approximately 30 percent, and receipts from exports fell from $426 million in 1977 to $184 million in 1985.[29] A structural adjustment program introduced between 1982 and 1985 failed to stem Tanzania's slide into economic crisis. President Nyerere resigned in 1985 and handed over the presidency to Ali Hassan Mwinyi, who launched an adjustment program in 1986.

Agriculture was not given many positive incentives but was expected to benefit from the reforms in the other sectors, especially their liberalization. As in Nigeria, agricultural performance improved modestly in the era of structural adjustment. Growth in agricultural GDP, which averaged 2 percent a year between 1978 and 1985, rose to 4.9 percent a year between 1986 and 1991, and the value of food sales increased 100 percent between 1983 and 1988.[30] However, it is misleading to read this improved

27. See Coulson (1975); Lofchie (1978); Mapolu (1973).
28. McHenry (1979, p. 212).
29. Husain and Faruqee (1994, p. 399).
30. Husain and Faruqee (1994, p. 399).

performance as the effect and the vindication of the structural adjustment program; it is better understood in relation to the self-interest of elites.

Self-interest led the elites to control agricultural production and the distribution and consumption of agricultural commodities through numerous institutions and regulations. But when these controls, often justified in the name of socialism, appeared to be choking the economy to death, the elites beat a retreat from control and liberalized. Liberalization brought some benefits to peasant producers, but that was incidental. What mattered was the survival and legitimacy of the political class, which would have been jeopardized by economic collapse. Structural adjustment was at best a peg on which to hang self-interest at a historical conjuncture. The policy must also be understood in terms of its latent and manifest functions; then one can see why the policy takes on a particular form and a particular content in a given situation.

Even under adjustment the contradiction between state and peasantry, between elites and masses, remains. Interests and politics define policies and the limits of agricultural performance. Significantly, the Tanzanian political class only backed off from controlling agriculture to avoid embarking on affirmative action to promote agricultural production. This situation continues to severely limit the development of agriculture. For instance, the input market remains "largely monopolistic, inefficient, and unresponsive to the needs of farmers."[31] The rural road networks so essential for agricultural development received little attention, and still less investment, so that by 1989 only 10 percent of the rural roads were in good condition. The roads are receiving some attention now only because of substantial funding from external donors.[32]

Overall, "agricultural services and infrastructure for poor farmers have not improved. Agricultural extension has been affected adversely by the general erosion of civil service salaries and shortages of government financing, trained personnel, and transport facilities. These problems were rampant well before the economic recovery program but have not lessened under the program, and in some intances they have deteriorated further. Rural roads continue to be deplorable, and transport networks for agricultural produce are inadequate and distributed unevenly throughout the country."[33]

To conclude, one cannot consider the prospects for agricultural development in purely economic terms. One must look at interests and their

31. Husain and Faruqee (1994, p. 406).
32. Husain and Faruqee (1994, p. 407).
33. Husain and Faruqee (1994, p. 408).

configurations and at the social location of actors and their politics, because those factors are decisive. Their significance is discernible even in many analyses undertaken by the World Bank; for example, in *A Strategy to Develop Agriculture in Sub-Saharan Africa and a Focus for the World Bank*.[34] It is interesting that most of the constraints on agricultural development discussed in the report are related to the dynamics of interest group competition and the politics of class, even though the report does not recognize the constraints in that way.

One constraint discussed is the poor state of roads and communications, a problem that the report links to "a heavy urban bias in most African public expenditure and policy regimes which has tended to focus transport infrastructure expenditures in large mega-cities which have little trade with rural areas, and which are dependent on imports. Secondary towns, which are collection markets for agricultural products, distribution points for farm imputes and places in which farmers children could seek secondary education, have often been neglected."[35]

Another major constraint, according to the report, is the tendency for governments to crush individual initiative at the farm and enterprise level by setting agricultural product prices too low and by maintaining overvalued exchange rates that effectively reduce the price of agricultural exports and agricultural products that compete with imports. In the vast majority of cases, African farmers have received only a fraction of the world price. Most recently, this situation has become much worse, since world prices for most agricultural commodities produced in Africa have fallen. Furthermore, agricultural stagnation is being perpetuated partly because "autonomous farmers' organizations and cooperatives, and farmer participation in the management of agricultural development was actively discouraged."[36]

Another impediment to agricultural development mentioned in the report is that "inadequate rural health, rural water, family planning, and educational facilities have resulted in a high incidence of relatively unhealthy, poorly educated people in rural areas, expanding in numbers at a high rate. Such people are less likely than better-educated, healthy people where numbers are expanding at a lower rate to innovate in agriculture and in agro-processing." Changes of land tenure systems are also compounding the problems of agricultural transformation: "Many governments have nationalized land. Some of this land is distributed for other uses, such as plantations owned by the state or by private enterprise

34. Cleaver (1993).
35. Cleaver (1993, p. 41).
36. Cleaver (1993, p. 41).

and farms owned by the elite. Both of these have reduced the traditional security of land tenure." Finally, in regard to the status of women, the report argues that for the African woman who is typically the African farmer and housekeeper, it is more difficult now "to maintain the required food production on increasingly smaller pieces of land. As forests recede, women must walk further for water as well. Increased work burdens on women make it difficult for them to apply the labour needed to intensify agriculture."[37]

The report strikingly illustrates the significance of class and power relations for agricultural development, providing insight into the clash between its latent and manifest functions.

Conclusion: The Problem of Agriculture

Appearances notwithstanding, the commitment of African leaders to agricultural development is problematic. The difficulty is not that they do not want agricultural development or that they are not attempting to bring it about. The difficulty is rather that their intentions and actions filter through complex layers of self-interest, and the policies that emerge effectively cease to be policies of agricultural development, as opposed to, for instance, strategies of survival, power, or accumulation.

To all appearances, agricultural policies in Africa have been dominated by the struggle of the political class against the peasantry over the control of the peasants' production and surplus. Such is to be expected in a continent whose leaders are seeking capitalist development in the context of largely precapitalist social relations of production. In most countries of Africa a stalemate seems to exist in the articulation between the capitalist and the precapitalist modes of production. The capitalist mode has become dominant but without accomplishing subsumption. It is this contradiction that the state and capital on the one hand, and the peasantry on the other, are acting out.

It has been argued in Goran Hyden's *Beyond Ujamaa in Tanzania* (1980), for instance, that development requires the liquidation, or at least the subordination, of the peasantry to the other social classes, that Africa's progress has been hampered by the persistence of what Hyden calls the "uncaptured peasantry." The behavior of the state in rural Africa might be seen in this context as a battle against the "insidious" freedom of the peasant, which is limiting the penetration of capitalism. Quite often, the

37. Cleaver (1994, p. 42).

process of capturing the peasant takes the form of repressive legislation. A conspicuous example is Nigeria's Land-Use Decree (1978), which vested all land in the government on the plea that doing so would facilitate the availability of land for development. What the decree has done is to give legal backing to the expropriation of the peasant farmer's land for other use.

Sometimes the methods of this struggle are much cruder. Thandinka Mkandawire is right in pointing out that African countries are behaving as though they have accepted the Hyden thesis that the African peasant must be crushed. As a result, there has been increasing social differentiation in the rural areas, land alienation and concentration through various schemes of "privatization," increasing subsumption of the labor process by capital, and a more repressive presence of the state apparatus in the rural areas.[38]

Since capital and peasantry are not in direct exchange relations, capital and state have to find other ways to control and appropriate peasant production. That may well be the main latent function of the measures paraded in Africa as policies and programs of agricultural development. They are arguably ways of controlling peasant production and appropriating surplus. Subsidized inputs, improved seedlings, agricultural credit and its inevitable "conditionality," quality control, extension services, and the lure of innovative technology can be used to determine what the peasant will produce and also how it is going to be produced and distributed.

Through these methods, the peasant has been steered to the production of industrial crops that local capital needs as inputs or to the production of what the state needs to earn foreign exchange. In addition, the peasant's surplus is regularly appropriated by complex mechanisms, to the disadvantage of rural producers—methods such as taxation, licensing, overpriced inputs, monopoly buying of produce, and differentials in producer and world prices.

The interests of the political elite underlie the turning of the internal terms of trade against peasants; the emphasis given to export crops even in the face of food shortages; the distribution of land in favor of those who do not put it to the most productive use; the use of agricultural support systems to control production and facilitate the appropriation of the surplus product; and the preference for large-scale capital-intensive projects, such as the irrigation schemes of the RBDAs, which offer poli-

38. Mkandawire (1987).

TABLE 3-2. *Agricultural and Population Growth Rates in Sub-Saharan Africa, 1970-92*[a]

Percent

Item	1970-80	1980-92
Agriculture	1.6	1.7
Population	2.8	3.0

SOURCE: Adapted from World Bank (1994c, pp. 165, 211).
a. Percents are weighted averages.

cymakers lucrative deals. These interests could allow the latent functions of agricultural policy to override its manifest functions. Insofar as that happens, the assumption of a continuing process of agricultural development becomes doubtful. It is not surprising that agricultural growth in Africa has been minimal, lagging behind population growth rates (see table 3-2).

Industrialization

Industrialization is beset by the same problems as agricultural transformation and by the same results. Like agricultural transformation, it often receives low priority. Its latent functions invariably clash with and override its manifest function. Initially, most African leaders had hoped that someone else would take on the burden of development, while they concentrated on the struggle for power and accumulation. Insofar as they showed interest in development, their overwhelming inclination was to move according to the contours of established colonial relations.

The first post-independence development plans in Africa—Nigeria's Development Plan, 1962-68; Kenya's First Development Plan, 1966-70; Tanzania's First Plan, 1964-69; Zambia's White Paper on Industrial Policy, 1964; Mali's Rapport sur le Plan Quinquennial de Développement Economique et Social de la Republique du Mali, 1961-1965—all assumed capital, technological, market, and management dependence. The Nigerian plan projected 50 percent of capital requirements from external sources; Tanzania's plan projected 78 percent of development expenditure to be financed externally. Like most African countries, Tanzania carried its financial dependence into the postcolonial era. The apparent resignation of African countries to dependence was as much a reflection of objective necessities as of subjective contingencies. To begin with, the dependence of the economies left hardly any room for maneuver. Tables 3-3, 3-4, and 3-5 tell the story of dependence and the limited leverage for endogenous development.

TABLE 3-3. *Tanzanian Development Budgets, 1948-61*
Thousands of U.K. pounds

Year	Capital expenditure	Reserves and other domestic sources	External grants	Loan funds
		Financed from		
1948	996	354	340	311
1952	4,989	1,985	1,080	1,924
1954-55	3,337	792	530	2,015
1955-56	4,084	1,136	677	2,271
1956-57	5,282	1,160	922	3,200
1957-58	5,454	1,668	899	2,887
1958-59	5,159	1,529	1,283	2,347
1959-60	3,939	852	1,361	1,726
1960-1	5,672	866	1,974	2,832

SOURCE: Republic of Tanzania (1964, p. 110).

The African successor to the colonial regime consisted not so much of a capitalist class as a mix of salaried persons and petite bourgeoisie: pensioners, lawyers, engineers, doctors, traders, teachers, ex-servicemen, journalists, religious leaders, farmers, small contractors, and trade unionists.[39] These were people whose political power did not have a strong economic base. They did not have confidence in their ability to manage a capitalist economy, especially one they did not control. Other groups in the society were likely to be even less qualified to manage.

Although the ability of the new rulers to manage economic development was doubtful, as well as their inclination to do so, we on the outside have readily assumed that Africa's ruling elites are bent on developing their countries. Our focus has been on the feasibility, success, or failure of African development projects, and particularly on how to improve their effectiveness.

But what is the country that is being developed? Who is doing this developing and why? Consider, for example, Nigeria. It is still a contested terrain of conflicting identities even after three decades of independence and a still longer period of being one political entity. Possibly some of Nigeria's elites think of themselves primarily as Nigerians and place their Nigerian identity above all other identities. But many more are ambivalent about what their primary identity should be. And even more place their Nigerian identity below that of their local community, nation, or ethnic group. In Nigeria, as in most African countries, the state remains a battleground where individuals fight for whatever power or resource they can

39. Coleman (1958).

TABLE 3-4. *Distribution of Trade in the Francophone Countries of Africa, including Madagascar, 1950–55*
Millions of dollars

Country or area	1950	1951	1952	1953	1954	1955
Imports						
France	317.8	488.9	467.5	409.3	475.6	467.3
Other French franc countries	34.0	51.9	52.1	48.4	57.5	64.4
Total, French franc countries	351.8	540.8	519.6	457.7	533.1	531.7
United Kingdom	7.3	11.4	21.6	17.1	19.2	18.7
Other sterling area countries	16.5	72.2	26.4	21.1	18.3	20.5
Total, sterling area	23.8	28.6	48.0	38.2	37.5	39.2
United States	43.6	38.9	43.4	27.9	28.8	38.5
Other dollar area countries	0.0	3.2	5.1	6.0	4.4	3.6
Total, dollar area	43.6	42.1	48.5	33.9	33.2	42.1
Nonsterling, non-French franc OEEC countries[a]	21.1	55.4	67.0	63.6	82.6	81.8
Other	24.9	12.6	21.3	16.4	18.9	20.2
Total	465.2	679.5	704.4	609.8	705.3	715.0

Exports						
France	234.3	294.5	302.7	318.6	380.4	333.0
Other French franc countries	24.5	42.7	43.2	52.5	52.4	49.1
Total, French franc countries	258.8	337.2	345.9	371.1	432.8	382.1
United Kingdom	9.7	9.0	5.6	9.7	13.9	14.1
Other sterling area countries	6.9	15.0	16.8	13.1	10.9	9.7
Total, sterling area	16.6	24.0	22.4	22.8	24.8	23.8
United States	8.9	11.1	12.8	18.3	45.5	51.1
Other dollar area countries	0.0	0.2	1.3	2.8	3.0	2.6
Total, dollar area	8.9	11.3	14.1	21.1	48.5	53.7
Non-sterling, non-French franc OEEC countries[a]	26.7	47.1	52.9	58.1	68.1	85.0
Other	23.4	5.3	9.2	11.5	10.5	9.2
Total	334.4	424.9	444.5	464.6	584.7	553.8

SOURCE: UNESA (1959, p. 177).
a. Organization for European Economic Cooperation, which became the OECD.

TABLE 3-5. *Principal Suppliers of Imports for Nigeria and Principal Customers for Its Exports and Re-exports, 1948-50, 1957-58*
Values are in millions of U.K. pounds

	1948-50		1957-58	
Country	Average annual value	Percent of total imports or exports	Average annual value	Percent of total imports or exports
Import supplier		Imports		
United Kingdom	29.2	54.0	69.4	43.5
Japan	5.0	9.0	18.5	11.5
West Germany	2.7	5.0	13.0	8.0
United States	3.2	6.0	8.9	5.5
Netherlands	1.2	2.0	8.4	5.5
Export customer		Exports		
United Kingdom	62.3	80.0	76.8	58.8
Netherlands	2.0	2.5	15.4	11.5
West Germany	0.4	0.5	8.5	6.5
United States	9.8	12.5	7.8	6.0
Italy	0.16	n.a.	7.4	5.5

SOURCE: Government of Nigeria (1959, p. 94).
n.a. Not available.

capture. In the struggle people may treat public office as a resource or appropriate public funds. Such behavior has led to comments about public corruption, lack of accountability, and absence of publicspiritedness in Africa, judgments that entirely miss the point.

Because of the historical legacy and objective conditions of contemporary Africa, a national development project in most African countries is not a rational undertaking. A few countries, such as Tanzania and Botswana, do have a fairly homogeneous culture, political integration, and leaders who have a credible sense of a national development project. But many more, such as Nigeria, Zaire, Uganda, Kenya, and Sudan, are so socially heterogeneous and politically fragmented from the exploitation of ethnic and other social differences that it is difficult to talk of a national development project. In some extreme cases, such as Zaire, the assumption of a development project and of a political leadership bent on development is patently absurd. In Zaire, as also in Togo, Somalia, and Sudan, rulership appears to be an exercise in "how to ruin a country."[40]

Nevertheless, all the leaders of Africa know they have to be seen to be assiduously promoting development. In most cases their efforts amount to little more than sporadic interventions that have been usually ineffective

40. Gerster (1989).

and unsustainable. Thus pursuit of industrialization in Africa has meant drifting from one received strategy to another in total indifference to historical specificity; each strategy is abandoned in turn as it falls victim to weak political will, the selfish interests of the agents of change, and hostile conditions at home and abroad.

Import Substitution

The first-generation development plans of post-independence Africa, following the patterns of colonial plans, emphasized infrastructure and the social sector rather than the productive sector. For instance, in Ghana's first full-blown post-independence plan—the Second Five-Year Plan, launched in 1959—the productive sector got only 20.3 percent of planned investment, while infrastructure and social services got 79.7 percent.

African leaders soon became dissatisfied with this manner of proceeding; they began to be conscious of the pervasive weaknesses arising from the lack of industrialization and the problems of dependence. Some were concerned about the deteriorating terms of trade, and many of them, conflating development with industrialization, were no longer so comfortable with remaining mere producers of primary commodities. The second-generation development plans began to shift emphasis to the productive sector and to grope for a strategy of industrialization. The first strategy adopted was import substitution.

In the 1960s manufacturing did grow considerably. In 1960 real manufacturing output for Sub-Saharan Africa was only 6 percent of GDP; between 1960 and 1965 its rate of growth was 9.3 percent a year, well above the growth rate of GDP.[41] From the middle 1960s, it declined steadily, and between 1975 and 1980 the growth rate became negative.

Despite the impressive growth rate of manufacturing from 1960 to the early 1970s, Sub-Saharan Africa did not keep up with growth rates in other developing areas. In that period Africa's share of global manufacturing value added rose from 0.7 percent to 0.8 percent. In contrast, between 1960 and 1975 the Latin American share rose from 4.1 to 4.8 percent, and the Asian share from 2.2 percent to 3.0. Africa's share of manufacturing exports fell from 1.1 percent to 0.6 percent between 1970–71 and 1975–76.[42]

It is interesting to look at the changes over time in the distribution of manufacturing production between the consumer, intermediate, and

41. World Bank (1983b).
42. Steel and Evans (1983).

capital goods of nine African countries engaged in import substitution (see table 3-6). In the early and mid-1960s, when African countries embarked on industrialization, simple consumer goods such as textiles, beer, beverages, and soap made the highest contribution to manufacturing output, a contribution that averaged 58.17 percent of total production. In the late 1970s it averaged 55.5 percent. The share of intermediate goods averaged 28.62 percent in the earlier period and 29.5 in the later one. The contribution of capital goods varied widely, from 1.1 percent for Ethiopia to 25.0 percent for Ivory Coast, and averaged 13.23 percent. By 1980 the contribution of capital goods still varied widely, from 2.3 percent in Ethiopia to 24.0 percent in Zimbabwe, for an average of 14.4 percent. Overall there was not that much change between the periods.

Looking at the import substitution experience of Kenya, Tanzania, and Zambia, one finds that all three countries expanded their manufacturing sector considerably between 1964 and 1977, with Kenya achieving the highest growth rate, 8.4 percent. But just what accounts for this growth? As table 3-7 shows, import substitution contributed an impressive 55 percent of manufacturing output for Zambia between 1965 and 1972. This was due not to export expansion but to local satisfaction of existing domestic demand. Following the Unilateral Declaration of Independence by Southern Rhodesia and the imposition of sanctions in 1965, Zambia had to find a means of obtaining locally the goods it had imported from Southern Rhodesia. Thus there was a sharp expansion in the production of textiles, leather, clothing, chemicals, and petroleum products.

In Tanzania, import substitution made no contribution to the expansion of manufacturing output in a similar period, a fact that is all the more surprising considering Tanzania's adoption of the philosophy of self-reliance. A trend that was perceptible in Kenya—namely, the simultaneous replacement and increase of imports—occurred in a more dramatic way in Tanzania. The import of textiles, clothing, beverages, and mineral products decreased by replacement,[43] but the import of other consumer goods, especially wood products and processed foods, rose just as fast. This process of neutralization was accentuated by the modest rise in the import of intermediate and capital goods (table 3-7).

It remains to consider the relation of import substitution to import dependence: to be specific, the extent to which manufacturing production depends on imported inputs (table 3-7). In Zambia, imported inputs as a percent of gross output (the import coefficient) decreased from 26 percent

43. Gulhati and Sekhar (1981).

TABLE 3-6. *Changes in the Distribution of Manufacturing Production in Nine Selected African Countries, Two Periods, 1960-67, 1974-80*[a]

Country and years considered	Earlier period (1960-67)			Later period (1974-80)		
	Consumer industries	Intermediates	Capital goods	Consumer industries	Intermediates	Capital goods
Value added						
Ghana (1962, 1979)	50.0	42.5	7.5	53.0	41.2	5.8
Zambia (1965, 1980)	43.9	34.0	22.2	40.8	35.5	23.7
Tanzania (1961, 1978)	74.0	23.0	3.0	57.0	35.0	8.0
Nigeria (1964. 1977-78)	54.5	36.3	9.4	42.4	34.4	18.1
Ivory Coast (1960, 1974)	50.0	25.1	25.0	63.1	18.2	18.9
Kenya (1960, 1980)	55.2	30.6	14.2	51.1	29.9	18.9
Zaire (1966, 1976)[b]	67.5	20.6	11.9	70.4	19.6	10.0
Gross output						
Zimbabwe (1965, 1978)	49.1	26.0	24.8	54.0	21.7	24.0
Ethiopia (1967, 1978-79)	79.4	19.5	1.1	67.7	30.0	2.3

a. "Consumer industries" comprise LSIC industry categories 31, 32, and 39; "intermediates" comprise industries 33-37; and "capital goods" consist of industry 38. Figures may not add to 100 percent because of rounding.

b. Constant 1976 prices.

TABLE 3-7. *Sources of Growth of Manufacturing Output and Import Substitution in Three African Countries, 1963-72*
Percent

Item	Kenya	Tanzania	Zambia
Source of growth			
Import substitution	17	-1	55
Domestic demand	70	96	44
Export demand	13	5	1
Period covered	(1963-71)	(1965-72)	(1965-72)
Manufacturing imports as percent of supply[a]			
1965	49[b]	56	66
1972	41[c]	57	47
Imported inputs as percent of gross output			
1964	20[b]	16[d]	26
1970	30[c]	14	18[e]

SOURCE: Gulhati and Sekhar (1981, p. 18).
a. Imports plus gross output
b. 1963.
c. 1971.
d. 1965.
e. 1969.

in 1964 to 18 percent in 1970. This change largely reflects input decline and value added in wood, textile, beverages, and metallic mineral and tobacco products. In Tanzania, the input coefficient fell by only 2 percent in the same period. Here the sharp decline of import dependence in consumer goods was offset by increasing import dependence in intermediate and capital goods. In Kenya, the import coefficient, far from falling, rose by 10 percent. There are two explanations for this: the importance of multinational corporations in the economy of Kenya, which often find it more profitable to procure inputs abroad from their own subsidiaries or associates, and by the higher share of intermediate and capital goods in Kenyan manufacturing.

To sum up the experience, constraints, and effects of import substitution strategy in Africa, the imports substituted tended to be very simple consumer goods such as textiles, beverages, and foods. Instead of moving on to intermediate and capital goods, African industrialization usually got trapped in the manufacture of simple consumer goods. In a few places the consumer goods share of manufacturing output actually increased rather than diminished. Africa achieved some increase in manufacturing output from the 1960s to the early 1970s without a significant change in its industrial structure.

In the course of import substitution, African countries become less dependent on imported consumer goods, but their dependence on imported intermediate and capital goods increased in the process, sometimes neutralizing the gains of reduced consumer goods imports and putting severe pressure on their balance of payments. The African experience of import substitution indicates that the strategy tends to run into difficulties after the initial period in which basic consumer goods are replaced. To move beyond consumer goods to intermediate and capital goods has been difficult for many reasons, including the nonavailability of capital and technological know-how and a preference for imported inputs. The East Asian countries that started with import substitution largely avoided these problems by greater discipline within the political class and business community, a better macroeconomic framework, and rapid movement toward an export push. This is well documented in the World Bank's *The East Asian Miracle* (1993).

The import substitution strategy was also greatly hampered by a limited domestic demand. Most African countries are too small and too poor to generate the demand to sustain continued industrialization on a scale that would offset the constraint of not being able to replace intermediate and capital goods. Exports might have been a way around this problem. But then the problems of protectionism in foreign markets and the competitive weakness of African exports would arise. It did not take long for Africans to discover the limits of import substitution and to recognize the need for a new approach to industrialization. But by then Africa's development problems had been compounded by the oil crisis, declining agricultural productivity (itself associated with an inappropriate industrialization strategy), deteriorating terms of trade, and escalating indebtedness.

I have followed convention and talked of import substitution. However, what was being practiced in Africa was not strictly speaking import substitution but rather import reproduction, which implies the domestic production of the particular product that was formerly imported and focuses on product-specific rather than generic functionality. It does not disaggregate the product into its cultural and aesthetic qualities and its function. Import substitution, on the other hand, makes this disaggregation in an effort to reach the "generic" character of the product, the purpose it serves, and the function it fulfills. Once that essence is grasped, a new product can be made to serve the function and yet be physically and aesthetically a much different product.

In being oriented to reproduction rather than substitution, Africa was taking on a more difficult task, which allowed for less flexibility and compounded the prospect of failure. But this choice should not be regarded as a simple one, reflecting the state of mind of policymakers. Rather, it is a choice historically and objectively constituted by the dependence of African leaders on the international development community and by the domination of African economies by multinationals.

Export Promotion

Export promotion was both a logical progression of import substitution and a reaction to its constraints. Foreign markets had to be found to deal with the problem of limited domestic demand and capacity utilization and to realize economies of scale. Because import substitution industrialization in Africa relied so heavily on imported inputs and the mobilization of capital to purchase machinery, it created a demand for foreign exchange. Export promotion was seen as a way to obtain the needed foreign exchange. As import substitution industrialization in Africa got under way, many countries found themselves producing too much relative to their capacity to import.[44] These were some of the circumstances that pushed African leaders into the export promotion route.

Export promotion appears to have been even less successful than import substitution. It was being pursued during a period of global export expansion, 1965 to 1973, when export volume in manufactured goods for the world as a whole was growing at 10.7 percent a year. For developing countries as a group, the growth rate was higher still, 11.6 percent a year. For Sub-Saharan Africa the growth of export volume in manufactures was 7.5 percent a year in 1965-73. Between 1973 and 1980 it declined to 5.6 percent a year; the decline continued in the period 1980-84, when it was only 2.9 percent a year. The growth rate rose in 1986, but by 1987 it had declined to −0.3 percent a year.[45]

In primary products, in which Sub-Saharan Africa is supposed to have comparative advantage, performance was just as bad. From 1965 to 1975 the growth of export volume of primary products for Sub-Saharan Africa was 15.3 percent a year. In 1973-80 it declined dramatically to −0.1 percent a year, and went down to −8.2 percent a year in 1980-84. For 1987 it was estimated at −7.4 percent a year. Africa is lagging not only behind other primary producers but also behind the industrialized countries.[46]

One might think that Africa's export drive would benefit from the

44. Killick (1978).
45. World Bank (1988).
46. World Bank (1988).

abundant supply of labor, labor intensity, and low wages. But African wages are relatively high compared with those of some other developing countries. At the same time, productivity is low, making it very difficult for African products to compete in the world market. This constraint, however, could have been reduced by suitable policies such as exchange rate adjustment.

Another obstacle to export promotion is the influence of multinational corporations in African economies. They offer some possibilities for export promotion, especially technical know-how, productive efficiency, and worldwide networks. But reliance on them tends to accentuate dependence, creating problems for the expansion of manufacturing and exports. Also, the multinationals tend to relate to Africa mainly as a source of raw materials and a market for manufactured goods. Processing natural resource-based commodities does not offer significant opportunities for export expansion either. As Ravi Gulhati and Uday Sekhar argue, "Many resource-based activities are very demanding of skills, capital and energy. Many are subject to sizable economies of scale. Some are subject to the monopolistic or oligopolistic control of trans-national corporations. Tariff rates in OECD markets tend to rise with the extent of processing, and shipping freight rates are frequently biased in favour of primary commodities."[47] In the face of these problems the export promotion strategy failed. That strategy, like import substitution, reinforces the tendency of African regimes to rely on the funds of the international development agencies and to follow the line of least resistance.

Some of these problems could have been overcome under different circumstances. But that did not happen because of weak institutions and failures of the political class, including indiscipline and corruption associated with the inability to engender a national development project and a strong sense of commitment to it. For instance, in Ivory Coast, Kenya, Nigeria, Ghana, and Zaire, the principle of promoting specific industries to encourage exports was subverted by parochialism and rent seeking and in Nigeria by large-scale projects such as the liquefied natural gas project. The Abeokuta Steel Mill failed because of corruption; basically the political elite tended to see such projects not so much in terms of the compelling need for national development as in terms of accumulation, patronage, and power. Again, the contrast to the performance of the East Asian political class is instructive.[48]

47. Gulhati and Sekhar (1981, pp. 30–31).
48. World Bank (1993b).

Indigenization

Some African countries, such as Nigeria, Ghana, Tanzania, and Senegal, considered indigenization of ownership and control of their economies as important aspects of industrialization. Under the influence of dependency theory, they saw an organic relationship between dependence and under-development. According to this view, dependence stands in the way of autocentric growth and tends to produce incongruities between the structures of production and consumption.[49] Indigenization was also moti-vated by nationalism. The independence movement was about the people taking control of their affairs, and the quest for development was integral to it. Foreign ownership and control of the economy was a constant reminder that the fulfillment of the nationalist aspiration had hardly begun. Indigenization was always on the agenda, albeit sometimes only implicitly.

Tanzania and Kenya

In Tanzania indigenization was pursued in the context of the parastatal system. That system came to dominate the economy in the wake of the Arusha Declaration, which committed Tanzania to socialism and self-reliance. In 1965 the National Development Corporation was founded to oversee the industrialization of Tanzania. It was the offshoot of the Tanganyika Development Corporation, founded in 1963. A system of paras-tatals was created for the financial sector, namely, the Tanzania Develop-ment Finance Corporation, the Bank of Tanzania, the Central Bank of Commerce, and the Tanzania Investment Bank. Agriculture was placed under two parastatals, the National Agricultural and Food Corporation and the National Agricultural Company. Retail came under the State Trading Corporation. By 1966 Tanzania had 43 parastatals and by 1973, 112.

The elaborate parastatal system in Tanzania projects a picture of an economy in which ownership and control have been localized. But that is more apparent than real. Consider the control of the parastatals them-selves. In 1967-70 external funds contributed 13 percent of parastatal expenditure. As Tanzania pursued indigenization and self-reliance, the external contribution to parastatal expenditure rose steadily and steeply: 20 percent in 1970-71, 56 percent in 1971-72, 73 percent in 1972-73, and 59 percent in 1973-74.

In Kenya the issue of indigenization assumed a special urgency for

49. Rweyemamu (1980).

reasons associated with settler colonialism. One factor making it so urgent was land hunger. The European settlers had reserved for their own use the best land in Kenya, 3 million hectares, or about 80 percent of the best land. Land hunger fanned the Mau Mau movement and the violent confrontation between Kenya and its colonizers. Under pressure from land-hungry Kenyans, the government launched successive schemes for buying out some of the Europeans' land for the settlement of Africans. The Million Acre Settlement Scheme of 1961 created African large-scale commercial farmers, or tried to create them. The settlement farms of this scheme were on the average 12 hectares and cost about KSh700 each. In 1965 another settlement was launched for smallholders, the Squatter Settlement Program; the average size of the farms under this scheme was 4.5 hectares.

While Kenya was indigenizing land ownership, its agriculture remained tied to foreign capital. According to Kenya's development estimates for the year 1971–72, of the total expenditure of KSh6,700,331 for agriculture, KSh4,399,099, or 59 percent, was to come from foreign sources. Of the estimated total crop production budget of KSh2,542,550, KSh1,610,010, or 63.3 percent, was to come from foreign sources. Of the gross total development budget of KSh2,393,070 of the Agricultural Development Corporation, the major agricultural credit agency of Kenya, KSh1,696,880, or 82.39 percent, was to come from foreign sources. The Agricultural Development Corporation expected 79.4 percent of its development expenditure from foreign sources.[50]

Kenya's pursuit of indigenization in commerce and industry was characteristically moderate. The government began by buying controlling shares in strategic businesses: 50 percent interest in the Standard Bank of Kenya, 50 percent in Barclay's, 60 percent in East African Oil Refineries, and 59 percent in East African Power and Lighting.

Kenya was wary of buying out foreign entrepreneurs to increase Kenya's control of the economy. The government reasoned that if the existing indigenous capital is used to buy foreign-owned enterprises, "the nation has no more productive assets than before, only their ownership has changed. What may be lost are the new resources that could have been purchased instead."[51] So indigenization was interpreted as a process to facilitate African business and commerce. To this end, the Industrial and Commercial Development Corporation (ICDC) was established; it stimulated African business mainly by offering credit facilities. It was

50. Ake (1985).
51. Government of Kenya (1965).

supported by a network of parastatals, notably the Development Finance Company of Kenya (DFCK), to help in matters of investment, the Kenya National Properties Limited (KNP) to help in procuring business premises, and the Kenya National Trading Corporation to assist Kenyans in retail and wholesale trade. These bodies not only contributed little to indigenous control of the economy; they created a problem in that they were not backed by a sound financial policy. Their preferred credit status placed considerable stress on the financial system.

As in agriculture, the bodies that were set up to bring about indigenization, especially the ICDC and DFCK, were themselves dominated by foreign capital. The Kenyan government had only a 15 percent equity share in both organizations, with the same proportion of shares going to the Commonwealth Development Corporation, the Netherlands Overseas Finance Company, and the German Development Corporation.[52]

Nigeria

Nigeria's commitment to indigenization was somewhat stronger. Nigeria was interested in using indigenization to localize ownership and control but also to further the transfer of technology and industrialization. The basic approach, carried through the Nigerian Enterprises Promotion Decrees of 1972, was to divide enterprises into two categories: one exclusively for natives, and the other in which foreigners could participate under certain conditions.

The exercise did not markedly increase Nigeria's control of its economy; the effect on the localization of ownership was more impressive. Essentially, what the decree achieved was to arrange an accommodation between indigenous and foreign capital; it reduced the chances of conflict and deepened the vested interest of the indigenous leadership in capitalism.

This accommodation often evolved into a partnership that tended to frustrate the purpose of indigenization. One problem of indigenization in Nigeria, and Africa generally, is the tendency for African entrepreneurs to become surrogates of foreign entrepreneurs in return for cash rewards or profitable business opportunities. The chairman of the Nigerian Enterprises promotion board, Minso Wadzama Gadzama, who was responsible for implementing the indigenization decrees, complained repeatedly of the collusion of Nigerians with expatriate business to defeat the decrees.

52. Ake (1985).

In an interview given to the *Business Times* in April 1982, he disclosed that Nigerians received money to buy shares as nominal owners. Having bought shares, they then pressed to retain the foreign management and even to increase the expatriate quota. Because of such collusion, Gadzama declared, more expatriates were involved in Nigerian enterprises five years after the indigenization drive began than before the decrees.[53]

Even when Nigerians used their own money to buy the expatriate enterprises, the new owners preferred profit to control. They wanted to retain the expatriate managers on the grounds that they were likely to perform better and make more profit. That was true even for those supposedly strategic enterprises in which the government acquired controlling interest. Usually the government settled for a division of labor in which the Nigerian managers were the staff management specialists such as legal advisers, personnel managers, and company secretaries, while expatriates held line management positions such as finance manager, manager, production manager and engineering manager.[54]

In the end, indigenization turned out to be only a strategy of incorporation; at best the indigenous political class improved the ownership of the economy but not its control. The drive for indigenization did not alter the division of labor between foreign capital and the indigenous political class, although it might have improved the access of the latter to business opportunities. Even that is uncertain, because in the course of implementing structural adjustment programs the indigenization measures have been largely reversed. The emphasis has shifted to providing incentives to attract foreign investment. Indigenization policies in Africa underline the inability or the reluctance of the African elite to take charge of economic management and development.

Conclusion

The indigenization process in Africa illustrates the ambivalence of the elites who make public policy and the clash between the latent and manifest functions of public policy. Even when indigenization was pursued in the context of a socialist policy, such as in Tanzania, it may have been successful in indigenizing ownership, but not control. Yet even if it had been successful in localizing control, the significance of this success would have been problematic. Control cannot be seen in isolation; it has to be related to other values, such as the effective management of the economy,

53. Ake (1985).
54. Ake (1985).

to maximize growth with equity. Often indigenization policies were carried out in a macroeconomic framework that did not serve the cause of economic growth or equitable distribution.

In sum, most of the indigenization drives in Africa invariably became a legitimizing veneer for the elites to sell public assets cheaply to themselves and to exploit those assets in ways that hurt the prospect of economic growth. Here again one recognizes the effects of class on the management of the economy.

Structural Adjustment

The international development community seems to have decided that structural adjustment is the way to recovery and sustainable growth. Although African governments and leaders disagree with the policy, they have had to go along with it. Africa has been adjusting for more than ten years, yet arguments about the merits and demerits of the program are still raging. The World Bank's 1994 comprehensive study, *Adjustment in Africa: Reforms, Results and the Road Ahead*, was supposed to have put an end to this debate. To all appearances it has not done so.

Are structural adjustment programs (SAPs) succeeding in Africa? The IMF is adamant that they are, as is the Bank, although it speaks less dogmatically. But judging by the narrow standards of the IMF, such as growth rate, external balance, and rate of inflation, it is difficult to make a case for structural adjustment, at least for Africa. The bottom line, as one student of adjustment argues, is that after a decade of structural adjustment there has not yet been one clear case of success.[55]

In evaluating structural adjustment, one needs to take account of the enormous significance that it has assumed in African economies and in the lives of Africans. Conceived originally as short-term measures for bringing a distressed economy back on course, SAPs now look like the only strategy of development in Africa, absurd as that may seem. Are the programs serving their goals in Africa? Since adjustment is a tool for a short-term objective, can it serve the broader objective of sustainable development? Are its social and political costs affordable? Most important, what is the significance of adjustment for development in Africa? And what is the significance of Africa's adjustment performance for my thesis that the current crisis of underdevelopment in Africa is essentially a political problem rather than an economic problem, although economic factors are not irrelevant?

55. Lancaster (1991–92).

Nigeria

Nigeria gives credence to the point that World Bank and IMF officials often make; namely, that whatever the problems of structural adjustment it is Africans who have created the need for it. Between 1973 to 1978, during Nigeria's first oil boom, oil revenue grew quickly, to more than 90 percent of Nigeria's export revenue. This increase was matched by an increase in public expenditure, which quadrupled between 1973 and 1975. By 1976 expenditure already exceeded revenue. During the second oil boom in 1979–85, the surge in oil revenue elicited such profligacy that real income began to decline rapidly, as much as 60 percent between 1980 and 1983, when Nigeria recorded a negative growth rate of −6.7 percent and a budget deficit rising to 13 percent of GDP. Austerity measures instituted in 1982 and 1984 failed, and the crisis deepened, especially with the sharp fall of real oil prices in 1986, the worsening of the terms of trade, debt service obligations, and a sharp fall in imports and exports. As mentioned in chapter 2, by the end of June 1986 a structural adjustment program was in place. The Nigerian adjustment program, which was typically eclectic and monetarist, had the following goals:

1. To diversify the productive base of the economy, reduce import dependence and dependence on oil.
2. To improve the balance of payments.
3. To improve public sector efficiency.
4. To give greater role to market forces and the private sector.
5. To facilitate accelerated, sustainable growth. These goals were to be achieved through:
   a. Fiscal and monetary policies to reduce inflation and ensure more rational and productive use of financial resources.
   b. Liberalization of price and exchange controls.
   c. Privatization and commercialization of public enterprises.[56]

The SAP designed by the government of Nigeria proposed trade liberalization; an import levy as a disincentive to imports; incentives for exports, especially non-oil exports; a reduction of the petroleum subsidy; privatization; and a balanced budget. The World Bank and IMF rejected this program, because it did not include the devaluation of the naira. The regime eventually adopted a revised SAP to meet that objection.

The major elements of the new adjustment program were implemented between July 1986 and December 1987, the most important being ex-

---

56. Husain and Faruqee (1994, p. 247).

change-rate adjustment. A floating exchange-rate system consisting of two tiers was established. The first tier was the official government-fixed rate for government transactions such as debt servicing; the second tier, funded by the government with petrodollars, was a market-determined tier in which foreign exchange was auctioned by the Central Bank of Nigeria (CBN). When the second tier became operational in September 1986, the naira was effectively devalued by 66 percent. The Nigerian government stayed with exchange-rate reform. According to the World Bank, "From 1988 to 1992, the quarterly average of the naira exchange rate per US dollar depreciated by 27 percent, 58 percent, 61 percent, and 83 percent over the 1987 base period." This devaluation was partly driven by the foreign exchange demand-supply gap, which continued to grow—from $360 billion in 1986, to $15 billion in 1989, to $17.5 billion in 1990.[57]

Another important reform in the Nigerian SAP was privatization, deemed necessary because the government was getting little from an investment of more than N23 billion in public enterprises. A committee was established to carry out this project. A decree of 1988 enjoined assessment of the possible privatization or commercialization of 145 public enterprises. Eventually most of these were scheduled for privatization. But implementation proved difficult, since problems arose with evaluation, the resistance of employees, and the auctioning of shares. By mid-1992 only 68 of these enterprises had been privatized, some only partially.[58]

The reforms also included measures to strengthen and discipline a market-driven financial system. In the reform period the financial system grew substantially. According to the CBN, commercial banks grew from 29, with 1,297 branches, in 1986 to 65, with 1,950 branches, in 1992. Merchant banks grew from 12, with 27 branches, in 1986 to 54, with 84 branches, in 1992.[59] The reforms also included interest rate deregulation and credit liberalization. A tight money policy was to be pursued to contain pressures for higher wages arising from the deflationary regime. The state and federal governments and their subsidiaries and parastatals were required to withdraw their deposits from the commercial and merchant banks and deposit them with the CBN. A credit ceiling was imposed, and credit targets were set. The manufacturing sector was to get 35 percent of commercial bank loans and 40 percent of merchant bank loans, while

57. Husain and Faruqee (1994, p. 256).
58. Husain and Faruqee (1994, p. 261).
59. Central Bank of Nigeria (1992).

agriculture was allocated 15 percent of commercial bank loans and 10 percent of merchant bank loans.[60]

Finally, the Nigerian SAP called for public service reform. The aim was to make the public service more professional, more accountable, and less prone to abuse of power and dereliction of duty. Ministers became chief executives and accounting officers in their ministries. The highest position in the ministry, the director-general, became a political appointment to be held at the pleasure of the president. The power of the Federal Government Service Commission to appoint, promote, and discipline was substantially diluted. The civil service was to be professionalized: every civil servant was to perform a specialized function; the idea of a central pool of civil servants and central deployment was to be discontinued. To improve their professional competence, public servants were to be trained on a systematic and continuous basis.

The political repercussions of SAP were a major concern, since Nigerians had debated and rejected an IMF loan tied to the adoption of the program. The concern was all the greater because civil society, especially mass organizations such as the labor movement and student groups, was developed and politically active in Nigeria. In these circumstances it was not surprising that special programs had been introduced to ameliorate the social impact of the SAP; notably, the establishment of the National Directorate of Employment to evolve measures for reducing unemployment, including training and placement and the provision of credit for small commercial and manufacturing enterprises; the urban mass transit programs, which provided buses and other vehicles to reduce the cost of public transportation; and the Directorate of Food, Roads and Rural Infrastructure, which tried to improve the delivery of social services in the rural areas and farmers' access to markets.

Even in the presence of these measures the demand for mitigating SAP's social effects continued to grow. In 1988 the federal government was obliged to introduce a reflationary budget and adopt a relief package, including a grant of N75 million to pharmaceutical companies for the importation of drugs to increase availability and reduce prices. A grant of N65 million was given to the National Directorate of Employment to facilitate youth employment. Also in 1989, the People's Bank was established, with a N270.5 million grant to give low-interest loans to small-scale enterprises. In 1990 the government encouraged the establishment of community banks to develop a financial system and improve the availability of credit in the rural areas.

60. Husain and Faruqee (1994, p. 254).

Has SAP succeeded in Nigeria? According to the World Bank study *Adjustment in Africa*, it has been moderately successful: "Nigeria's adjustment program had a positive impact on aggregate output. By 1988 output rebounded from its limited 2 percent growth in 1986 to growth at almost 9 percent, spurred primarily by an increase in agricultural production. Between 1989 and 1991 overall GDP growth averaged 5.8 percent annually, dominated by the oil sector."[61]

This "robust growth of GDP" occurred despite what the study considers a reform process that has generally been "unsatisfactory." The study explains it as follows: "Oil production and experts are not affected by public sector inefficiency and other policy distortions," by the performance of the private sector, especially the agricultural sector, and by better utilization of capital as well as increasing investment.[62]

Agriculture seems to have responded positively to structural adjustment, with output growing "by more than 4 percent in the five-year post-adjustment period compared with near stagnation in the five-year period before adjustment."[63] According to statistics of the Central Bank of Nigeria, which the World Bank study also cites, between 1986 and 1990 the production index for export crops (with 1980 as base year) was 141.8, and the real price index was 159.4. For food crops the production index was more impressive still, 183.8, but the real price index was only 86.4. The Bank study explains this highly significant anomaly by saying that "such non-price factors as the availability of imported technology, improved infrastructure and the weather may be more important determinants of the difference."[64]

Manufacturing production is also judged to have benefited from adjustment, growing at an average of 5.1 percent over the adjustment period 1986–91, from a negative growth rate of -3.9 percent in 1986. Nevertheless, this is hardly a sterling performance, given the generous foreign allocation and other concessions to the manufacturing sector. Despite such incentives, the contribution of manufacturing to GDP remained a mere 8.3 percent. Indeed, the SAP has caused a shift from production to services. While the contribution of manufacturing to GDP was stagnating, that of finance and insurance rose from 3.11 percent in 1986 to 8.7 percent in 1991.

SAP does not appear to have helped much in regard to external balance

61. Husain and Faruqee (1994, p. 264).
62. Husain and Faruqee (1994, p. 264).
63. Husain and Faruqee (1994, p. 273).
64. Husain and Faruqee (1994, p. 273).

and the diversification of the Nigerian economy. Total merchandise exports fluctuated during the adjustment period, rising from $6.8 billion in 1986 to $13.9 billion in 1990 and then falling to $12.1 in 1991. These fluctuations were not due to SAP but to the oil sector. Non-oil exports did not increase markedly as had been expected. In 1992 non-oil exports accounted for a negligible 3.6 percent of export earnings, while the share of oil was 77.3 percent.

The indebtedness of Nigeria has increased over the adjustment period. The debt stock, which was only $18.9 billion before the SAP period, had risen to $33.2 billion by 1991. It fell to approximately $28 billion in 1992 as a result of a buy-back arrangement with the London Club. But by 1994 it had again risen beyond the 1991 level to nearly $40 billion. Exchange-rate management under SAP has been disappointing in its effects. Inflation, which averaged 18 percent between 1980 and 1985, rose to an average of 24 percent between 1986 and 1991; by the end of 1992 it was over 46 percent and remained in that high range through 1993. The World Bank study blames government policies, which supposedly defeated the purpose of SAP: "The fiscal and monetary restraint envisaged by the structural adjustment program was either abandoned or not pursued vigorously from the outset. Credit to the federal government increased by 12 percent in 1987. Although net foreign assets fell by 39 percent, net credit to the private sector remained relatively strong, all of which increased the supply of money by 23 percent in 1987."[65]

And despite the measures taken to cushion the impact of structural adjustment, its social consequences were severe, especially for the poor: "Employment in the manufacturing sector declined despite increased output and low wages because private firms have streamlined operations in order to control operating costs. The overall structure of employment has changed, with the greatest decline evident among expatriate employees and unskilled workers. With the contraction in formal sector employment, the informal sector appears to have grown."[66]

The poor have suffered from the high rate of inflation as well as from other conditions: the fall in real wages among urban workers; the collapse of infrastructure, including water supply, electricity, and transportation; the new commitment to cost recovery in education, health care, and City Council services; and the general decline in welfare indicators such as adult literacy rate and primary school enrollment. Throughout the adjustment period SAP continued to be resented and was a constant cause of unrest,

65. Husain and Faruqee (1994, p. 266).
66. Husain and Faruqee (1994, p. 277).

especially among the working class, which effectively opposed its intensification, particularly the total removal of the petroleum subsidy.

In this brief review of structural adjustment in Nigeria, I have evaluated the SAP regime by the narrower criteria of the World Bank and IMF and have greatly relied on the data from these institutions. Even by those standards the SAP regime could hardly be called successful. It seems even less so when it is evaluated from broader concerns. But before going into those concerns, I review the Ghana experience of structural adjustment.

Ghana

The Bretton Woods institutions regard Ghana as "the front-runner in adjustment," the clear success story of the adjustment regime in Africa. In *Adjustment in Africa* the author of the Ghana chapters says: "By customary criteria, Ghana's adjustment program has been a success. Policy reform has been extensive, despite opposition and institutional constraints. The benefits of adjustment have been large, visible, and widely shared. The results are all the more remarkable given the chaotic initial conditions and the external shocks sustained since it began."[67]

The economic condition of Ghana in 1983, when it started its adjustment program, was very poor. Major physical infrastructure and public facilities were at different stages of decay or collapse. Shortages of basic commodities, including food, were widespread. Even while Ghana was reeling from one of the worst droughts in its history, nearly 1 million Ghanians living in Nigeria were forced to return home. Cocoa prices were falling, and government revenues had been declining for several years, as had incomes in real terms. Cocoa production had fallen from 376,000 tons in 1975 to 179,000 tons in 1983, and government revenue had fallen from 20 percent of GDP in 1970 to only 5 percent in 1982. These two declining values were related. Cocoa production was declining partly because cocoa producers were being so overtaxed that they only received, according to the World Bank, between 15 percent and 40 percent of prevailing world prices. In the face of this disincentive, farmers produced less and depressed government revenue. While productivity and incomes fell, inflation increased phenomenally at an average annual rate of 53 percent for the decade before adjustment, 1972–82.[68]

Like most adjustment programs in Africa, exchange-rate adjustment was a central element in Ghana's SAP. A series of drastic devaluations

67. Husain and Faruqee (1994, p. 153).
68. Husain and Faruqee (1994, p. 159).

reduced the cedi's exchange rate to the dollar from ¢2.75 in 1983 to ¢90 in 1986. More devaluation was to follow. Ghana has had one of the most drastic exchange-rate adjustments in the history of policy reform.

Ghana's adjustment program paid much attention to the liberalization of trade. An important part of this process was the liberalization of price controls and foreign exchange regulations. Import taxes were substantially reduced, though by 1992 they were still roughly 10 percent across the board. Export was liberalized and encouraged by a system of incentives, including tax rebates on export earnings and duty-free concessions for certain imports, especially machinery.

Along with trade, the financial sector was liberalized. Interests rates were deregulated for commercial lending, and government divested itself of the ownership of commercial banks. Commercial banks were no longer required to meet specific quotas for sectoral lending and left commercial credit to market forces. In effect, government shifted from control of the financial sector to indirect influence by means of such instruments as government securities.

As regards agriculture, which accounts for more than 40 percent of the country's GDP, the emphasis of the reform program was less on positive intervention than on government withdrawal and on the salutary impact of exchange-rate adjustment in increasing the prices of traded agricultural commodities. Government subsidies to agricultural production, especially fertilizers and other imports, were removed. At the same time, government divested itself of agricultural ventures, including fertilizer production. Export trade restrictions in agriculture, especially export taxes, were reduced. New export arrangements for agricultural exports gave Ghanian farmers a higher proportion of prevailing world prices for their exports.

The adjustment program of Ghana, like that of Nigeria, was sensitive to the social consequences of adjustment. The Bretton Woods institutions were particularly interested in the social consequences of SAP in Ghana, since that country was regarded as the model pupil that would help to vindicate structural adjustment programs throughout Africa. As a result, the level of foreign aid to support the adjustment regime in Ghana was unusually high. According to *Adjustment in Africa*, foreign aid to Ghana rose from $270 million in 1984 to $480 million in 1990.[69] Adjustment support enabled Ghana to undertake in 1988 a rather ambitious program of action for mitigating the social consequences of adjustment, called

69. Husain and Faruqee (1994, p. 172).

PAMSCAD. This ambitious and complex measure, which involved "seven sectoral ministries, thirteen public agencies, twenty-three distinct projects and numerous designated activities," did not succeed:

> The intent was to provide quick relief to the poor throughout the country. While some progress was made, the impact was less than anticipated. The difficulty in targeting assistance to the poor stems from two factors. First, the poor are not concentrated in any particular area. Second, their consumption pattern does not differ distinctly from the pattern of the nonpoor. Furthermore, most of the measures under the program of action attempted to overcome some of the shortcomings of similar programs implemented elsewhere. For example program design called for avoiding simple transfers in favor of producing useful assets for local communities. In addition, the wages offered under the project were kept relatively low to avoid attracting the nonpoor. But these constraints generated new problems. Administrative procedures became cumbersome, and the response rate from the poor was lower than expected.[70]

Still, the Bank insists that adjustment has not harmed the poor but made them better off. The study says that some quality-of-life indicators such as infant mortality were positive during the adjustment period. It also asserts that agricultural policy liberalization has helped the poor by improving farmers' earnings.

Perhaps it is an indication of the magnitude of the problems of structural adjustment in Africa that the Bretton Woods institutions regard Ghana as their star pupil. Ghana's performance is hardly outstanding even by their own evaluation:

> The adjustment program has clearly changed the economy. Growth has been restored. Since 1983 real income per capita has averaged 2 percent annually—in contrast to the 1970s when real income fell by a third. Evidence suggests also that the benefits of growth have been distributed broadly. Farmers and rural workers have benefited from improved producer prices for cocoa and the liberalization of trade for other cash crops. Real food prices (for cereals and roots) have fallen gradually. Furthermore, government expenditures on social programs rose significantly during the adjustment period. Social indicators show improvements across the board.

70. Husain and Faruqee (1994, p. 185).

The extent and replicability of Ghana's experience have attracted much interest. Many believe that Ghana's adjustment performance has been exceptional by regional standards. But the performance largely reflects the depth of economic decline before reform. Over a longer time horizon, Ghana's record is not that distinctive. For example, between 1980 and 1990, real GDP growth in Ghana averaged 3 percent annually, behind nine other sub-Saharan African countries, including Botswana, Burkina Faso, Burundi, Congo, Mali and Mauritius and comparable to six others, including Malawi, Senegal, Tanzania and Zimbabwe.[71]

A serious problem raised by the Ghana experience is whether the gains of structural adjustment, especially economic growth, can be sustained. This question is particularly serious not only because Ghana is regarded as the success story in Africa but also because it was given an unusual level of foreign aid to mitigate the rigors of structural adjustment and to ensure that the gains of adjustment would be sustained.

Ghana's GDP growth rate averaged close to 5 percent a year over the adjustment period, and the economy expanded by about 40 percent. Approximately 77 percent of this growth, according to the World Bank study, was in the service sector, particularly commerce. Industry accounted for only 18 percent of the growth, and of this, 3.6 percent was from mining activities. More significant, in an agricultural economy, agriculture accounted for only 5 percent of the growth. The growth pattern, normal by standards of highly industrialized countries, clearly indicates a serious weakness, namely, that the Ghana economy is not being adjusted in a way conducive to sustainable growth. The study takes note of this and suggests "a need to re-examine policy and other structural constraints."[72] These structural constraints and weaknesses include a rudimentary financial system and a capitalist class. The rate of domestic saving rose only slightly, from 5 percent to 8 percent of GDP, compared with a current Sub-Saharan Africa average rate of 13 percent. Ghana has nonetheless been able to achieve an investment rate of 16 percent of GDP. This means that much of the investment has come from foreign aid, largely for government investment and investment by public enterprises. The World Bank study estimates that private sector investment is no more than 8 percent of GDP and is properly concerned about that: "After a decade of generally favourable adjustment efforts, private sector invest-

71. Husain and Faruqee (1994, p. 155).
72. Husain and Faruqee (1994, p. 170).

ment, normally the driving force for vigorous growth, has not been particularly strong."[73]

Adjustment, Growth, and Development

Structural adjustment in Africa has become the surrogate of a role it cannot possibly fulfill. By its nature the structural adjustment program is an interim measure; it is more like first aid in the face of an emergency, not a cure. More important, the structural adjustment program is not a development strategy. It is supposed to be a response to economic shocks and salient imbalances, a way to remove distortions and constraints of economic growth, not a recipe for economic growth.

By all indications, the Bretton Woods institutions and all the proponents of SAPs know this. They do not claim that SAP is other than an emergency measure, nor do they claim that it is a strategy of economic development. But they have, inadvertently perhaps, perpetuated such misrepresentations. They have failed to put anything other than SAP on offer in Africa for well over a decade, during which they have been absorbed in the advocacy and practice of SAP while remaining mute on development strategy. African critics of SAP have not helped matters. Even while viewing SAP negatively, they have kept it current. They are trapped in its discourse; most important, they have offered no alternative to SAP as an emergency measure or as a credible alternative development strategy. Apart from minor modifications of SAP, such as some sensitivity to its social consequences, all that African critics have achieved is to give SAP an even stronger and more ubiquitous presence.

In recent times the tendency is to regard SAP as part of the hegemony of the market following the winding down of the cold war and the collapse of the Soviet empire. The market is revered as the key to the wealth of nations. Some people, impressed by its role in material civilization, are now inclined to represent it as the truth of history. In this context, it is not surprising that the wealthy industrialized countries have taken the position that what the poorer countries need to overcome their economic backwardness is to embrace the market. The industrialized countries all support SAP as the response to the crisis of underdevelopment and as the way to generate the movement to the market. For that reason the question of development strategy no longer seems to arise. The issue of

---

73. Husain and Faruqee (1994, p. 175).

how development should proceed, at least in broad outline, has been settled.

The settlement of the issue is more apparent than real, however. The market cannot be and never has been a strategy of economic growth, even in the experience of the North. The North, exercising the prerogative of victory in the long-drawn-out contest of paradigms of society, has reinvented development as an ideological emblem. The history of economic growth in the North has been sanitized and recast as a celebration of the North. The rigors of primitive accumulation and the process of proletarianization have been glossed over, as have the contradictions of the market that bred statism and the welfare state, without which capitalism may well have collapsed. Also forgotten is colonialism and its contribution to economic development.

What now exists is a simplified view of economic development, which posits that underdevelopment was initially universal and that every country can grow out of it by following policies that are known, tested, and unfailing. Thus the late starters are saddled with the singular burden of carrying out an abstract and misleading conception of development that does not reflect the realities of their own history or even the histories of the North. Because Africa, in particular, is guided by fictitious concepts and is working with blunt instruments, its social transformation has been unduly difficult.

One of the greatest drawbacks of SAP is its politics, which is typically authoritarian. Perhaps that was inevitable in Africa. There the SAP regimes started before the wave of democratization; a basis hardly existed for subjecting SAP to a democratic mandate. The African leaders whose performance had contributed to the need for adjustment were neither in the habit of subjecting public policy to democratic determination nor willing to expose their governance record to public debate. In any case, by the time SAP became an issue, they had invariably run out of options. The international supporters of SAP were scarcely more inclined to the democratic legitimation of public policy. For one thing, they had near-absolute faith in the validity of their policy prescription; for another, they assumed that the austerity of SAP would not survive a public debate. As a result, the internal and external promoters of SAP were disposed to its authoritarian imposition.

This attitude compounded the problems of Africa immensely. SAP became necessary in the first place because of the extreme economic deterioration that had depressed real incomes and the quality of life and subjected the political and social system to much stress, including alienation, an intensifying struggle for a diminishing surplus, and an increase in the incidence of violent conflict. But SAP in effect accentuated those tendencies.

Although I suggested above that the politics of SAP is authoritarian, strictly speaking, SAP has no politics. Rather, the program hinges on the renunciation of politics—politics understood as the process of aggregating interests, articulating them, and negotiating consensus on the general thrusts of public policy and on the managers of public policy. But as seen, SAP usually arrives in Africa by imposition. This imposition calls for considerable coercion because the government doing the imposing has no legitimacy and because African SAPs are extremely austere. With rare exceptions, SAP goes hand in hand with the militarization of society. A society thus militarized may look superficially unified and stable in its monolithism, but it is effectively fragmented, incoherent, and unstable.

This political incoherence is the bane of Africa. The state in the sense of a public force or a truly public sphere, a commonwealth or res publica, hardly exists except in a few instances. In much of Africa, the public sphere is a contested space where strangers converge to appropriate for their interest groups whatever is on offer, including the power of the state. Every interest group is out for itself; each wants to appropriate and privatize state power to its own benefit. The issues of national interest, public interest, or even public policy scarcely arise. When they exist, they are lost in the contradiction between the manifest and latent functions of policy.

How so much of Africa got that way is a very complicated problem that can only be touched upon here. The problem clearly has something to do with the forms of social heterogeneity that exist in Africa. But that is not enough, because similar conditions exist in countries such as India and Indonesia, where the political elites have been coherent enough to launch a development project. Africa's political incoherence has something to do with authoritarianism, which has engendered strong centrifugal tendencies. Again, one has to go deeper to find intervening variables to account for the fact that countries like Taiwan, Singapore, China, and South Korea have found the political coherence to effectively execute a development project. But for now my limited concern is to show that structural adjustment has contributed to the political incoherence in Africa.

In Nigeria, for instance, structural adjustment was a major cause of the chain of political crises that has shaken the country since 1988, beginning with the political crisis of the SAP debate itself. The very tabling of the debate caused considerable anger and alienation from the public, which was merely reminded of the economic mismanagement that necessitated SAP in the first place. The proposal to adopt SAP was angrily rejected, but a government that had clearly run out of options and out of legitimacy imposed it anyway.

SAP deepened the division between the military and civilians, and between ethnic groups as elites invoked ethnic identity. Regionalism and religious differences became politicized as elites came under pressure to find a base of power at a time of political anxiety and economic crisis. These differences raised the premium on political power and the intensity of political competition. Politics became overcharged and lawless as efficiency norms replaced legitimacy norms. Attempts to conduct party primaries broke down in disorder. When a presidential election was finally held, the military annulled it because its outcome was too threatening to the prevailing structure of power. Nigeria fell into deep political crisis: two presidents disputing political legitimacy, most nationalities demanding a sovereign national conference to reconsider the basis of political association in Nigeria, several groups seeking a confederation, and a few clamoring for secession.

A grave defect of SAP is that it is blind to its own politics, not only about its impact on politics but also about the impact of politics on its own feasibility. In particular, SAP is blind to the fact that it is usually associated with the de-democratization of politics. In Nigeria SAP was established in the wake of a military coup and, as mentioned, after rejection of the outcome of a public debate that had come down heavily against structural adjustment. In Ghana structural adjustment followed the shift from the populist program of the Provisional National Defense Council (PNDC) in 1982–83 to a conservative posture in 1983, when President Jerry Rawlings, alarmed by a collapsing economy and prompted by the IMF, veered to the right and purged the PNDC, appointing to it conservatives such as Justice Anan and replacing the People's Defense Committees, the radical grass-roots bodies that were the soul of the populism of 1982, with Committees for the Defense of the Revolution, which were state controlled and had largely an economic role. In Burkina Faso adjustment came after the shift from Thomas Sankara's democratic revolution to the conservative coup of Blaise Campaore in October 1987. Campaore abolished the Comités de Défense de la Révolution, which epitomized people's power in the Sankara revolution, and restored the power of technocrats and bureaucrats and the status of traditional rulers. To be sure, structural adjustment was subjected to some consultation, but that was a carryover from the Sankara legacy, neatly exploited to legitimate the shift to the right.

Because SAPs in Africa tend to be associated with de-democratization and a shift to the right, it is difficult to sustain the view that structural adjustment favors the poor or the expectation that its social impact will be effectively cushioned. True, the rural poor, especially farmers, could benefit from some aspects of deregulation such as the dissolution of commodity boards and the deregulation of prices. But these are incidental benefits that do not change the point: the undemocratic politics of SAPs cannot privilege the poor; it is more prone to marginalize or victimize them.

But the fate of the poor is not the main issue here. The main issue is the association of structural adjustment with de-democratization and political incoherence. These tendencies stand in the way of evolving consensus on a development project and a development strategy; they prevent the people from possessing their own development strategies and development policies.

Conclusion

To return to the larger picture: this chapter has elaborated on the argument that the problem is not so much that the development project in Africa has failed as that, because of bad political conditions, it never really got started. The point is not that there are no development strategies, policies, and projects, but rather that they are produced by a particular government in office and a particular elite in power in the context of a determinate state and a historical configuration of social forces. However, because of the constitution of the state in Africa and the dynamics of social forces, these policies and projects tended to be mere gestures whose latent functions have overriden their manifest functions. With few exceptions, the African elites have been more interested in political survival than in development, and the conditions of their survival have usually been inimical to development. Agriculture has not been given the importance it deserves, and agricultural policy and development have tended to disappear in the struggle between the state and political elites, who want to control the peasants' surplus product, and the peasants, who resist expropriation.

Political elites absorbed in the struggle for survival and often lacking in cohesiveness and confidence have largely ceded development strategy to external agents, but in exogenizing development they also aborted it. Nonetheless, gestures continue to be made toward development as African leaders adopt ad hoc, and often opportunistically and confusedly, the latest fad of the international development community—import substitution, export promotion, integrated rural development, structural adjustment, and so forth—with little concern for the realities of African conditions. These are passing enthusiasms, not development strategies. And now Africa is stuck in the discourse and practice of SAP, which is only an emergency measure rather than a development strategy, and there is no sign of anything else on the menu.

4

Blocked Options

Grand strategies of development are now of less interest than specific policy options. Amid considerable confusion over just what the problem is, there exist many options on how to proceed. In what follows I examine some of these options in order to show how they are politically constituted and why, despite their popularity and apparent feasibility, they are blocked.

The International Environment

In the past it was assumed that the international order would not change in any way significant for the pursuit of development in Africa. The winding down of the cold war has altered that assumption. Now there is great concern among Africans and some members of the international development community about the marginalization of Africa. And for good reason. The considerable attention that Africa enjoyed in the 1960s and 1970s owed much to the cold war. Africa, like every other region of the developing world, was courted for diplomatic support. Even those parts of Africa with limited strategic, political, and economic attraction were courted as each side in the cold war—principally the United States and the Soviet Union—tried to limit the influence of the other side in the world and to expand its own.

Each side cared deeply whether African countries took the socialist or capitalist path, for that choice had some potential for making the world safer or more hostile to it. More important, each side thought that its acceptance as a model by any developing country would help to vindicate its worldview. This courtship of Africa was not limited to the superpowers, however. The cold war contributed to some localized rivalries, such as those between North and South Korea, East and West Germany, Israel and the Arabs. The principals in these rivalries also cultivated allies in Africa, enabling Africa to get into many more foreign policy agendas.

All that has changed now that the cold war is over. It is difficult to envisage anything that can keep Africa on the international agenda. It cannot be Africa's needs or humanitarian interest; it has to be something that matters significantly for the economic, political, and strategic interests of the major international players. The problem of sustaining any interest in Africa is compounded by the dramatic changes resulting from the disintegration of the Soviet empire, changes that have captured the imagination of the world.

Africa is apparently being marginalized by developments in science, technology, and production that are unlinking the industrial economies from the primary economies. Primary products are being displaced by synthetic materials, which are often stronger, more versatile, and easier to work with. At the same time the raw material content of goods has been decreasing in a continuing process of dematerialization and miniaturization.

These changes mean that the highly industrialized countries are not as dependent on primary producers as they used to be. These objective factors, more than the deliberate manipulation of the world market, are undermining primary producers, depressing commodity prices, diminishing their exports and export earnings, turning the terms of trade against them, and driving most of them ever deeper into debt. Whether they are anybody's fault or not, these changes objectify the North-South divide and the marginalization of Africa.

In the past, African leaders put great effort into development through internationalism, thinking perhaps that this would be a useful way of getting resources from the industrialized countries while diversifying their dependence enough to find some space for maneuver. This approach was tested in the demand for a new international economic order, which accomplished nothing.

More interesting perhaps because of its African specificity was the effort to pressure the international community through the United Nations to help Africa out of its crisis. By 1984 African countries recognized that their economic decline was so deep that it had created an emergency that must be tackled. Consultations were held among African leaders in the context of organizations such as the United Nations Economic Commission for Africa (UNECA), the Economic Community of West African States (ECOWAS), the Organization of African Unity (OAU), and the African Development Bank (ADB). At the same time pressures started to mount for a special session of the UN General Assembly on the African crisis. Eventually these pressures prevailed.

As noted in chapter 2, in anticipation of the special session, African countries prepared a comprehensive document called *Africa's Submission to the Special Session of the United Nations General Assembly on Africa's Economic Crisis*. The program of action in this document, known as Africa's Priority Program for Economic Recovery, 1986–90 (APPER), was approved in 1985.

The special session in 1986 welcomed the APPER affirmation that Africans took "responsibility for the economic and social development of their countries, identified areas for priority action and undertook to mobilize and utilize domestic resources for the achievement of those priorities." The General Assembly went on to adopt its own program, the United Nations Program of Action for African Economic Recovery and Development, 1986–1990 (UNPAAERD). To emphasize its seriousness, Resolution S-13/2 urged the UN secretary-general to monitor the implementation of UNPAAERD and report back to the General Assembly at its forty-second and forty-third sessions.

In a special report on UNPAAERD in 1991, Secretary-General Javier Pérez de Cuéllar showed the inadequacy of the response of the international community to the program. Its support was expected to come through greater official development finance (ODF), especially official development assistance (ODA).

The report lamented that "there was a reduction, rather than an increase, in real net resource flows to Africa" by the end of the period of UNPAAERD. Measured in 1986 prices and exchange rates, net resource flows declined from $24.6 billion in 1986 to $23.3 billion in 1990.[1] ODA was essentially stagnant for the period at $16.2 billion in 1986 and $16.9 billion in 1989. The net flow of export credits declined sharply, from $2.1 billion in 1985 to -$1.8 billion in 1988. Private flows fell from $5.3 billion in 1986 to an estimated $3 billion in 1990.[2]

Although the prospects of promoting development in Africa through multilateralism have become more utopian, the international development community continues to argue for international partnership in development and in some cases, such as the Lome Convention, tries to make its usefulness to Africa plausible. This tendency finds willing collaboration among African leaders, some of whom are so hard pressed that they are easily seduced by any arrangement that promises some transfer of

1. World Bank and USAID (1991, p. 31).
2. World Bank and USAID (1991, p. 31).

TABLE 4-1. *Financial Resources Available from the Lome Convention, 1975-95*

Millions of ECUs

Convention	Year	Amount
Lome I	1975-80	3,450
Lome II	1980-85	5,700
Lome III	1985-90	8,500
Lome IV	1990-95	12,000

SOURCE: European Commission (1994, p. 9).

resources, however meager. But as can be seen from the Lome Convention, such arrangements are not a development option.

The Lome Convention, a comprehensive cooperation agreement between the European Community (EC) and African, Caribbean, and Pacific Countries (ACP), is negotiated through three institutions, the ACP-EC Council of Ministers, the ACP-EC Committee of Ambassadors, and the ACP-EC Joint Assembly. The convention was signed in 1975 and then renewed in 1979, 1984, and 1989. The agreements give aid to the ACP countries through several funds; namely, Emergency Aid; Refugee Aid; Sysmin, for mining industries; Structural Adjustment Fund, for policy reform; and Stabex, for stabilizing earnings from agricultural exports. They also offer trade assistance such as some duty- and quota-free access to EC markets and special funds, mainly the European Development Fund (EDF) and the European Investment Bank (EIB).

There are some real benefits in these arrangements. But they are small and their cost is high, sometimes arguably prohibitive. To begin with, the amount of money that the European Community puts out for the Lome Convention is quite small relative to the number of years covered, the number of countries to be served, and the needs of the ACP countries, and even to the number of countries that are collectively giving this aid. For instance, under Lome I the financial outlay was ECU3,450 million (European currency units) for five years, or ECU690 million a year for all ACP countries (see table 4-1).

Lome IV (1990-95) was hailed as a watershed in the financial outlay of the EC for Lome. Compared with Lome III (1985-90), it increased total aid nominally by about 40 percent and by about 20 percent in real terms. But ECU12,000 million for five years of Lome IV comes to ECU2,400 million a year for all ACP countries from the entire EC. And some of this money will be recycled back to the donors through tied purchases and technical services.

One of the most important benefits of the Lome Convention to the

ACP countries is supposed to be preferential treatment. A World Bank and U.S. Agency for International Development report argues that "these preferential arrangements have not resulted in marked increases in African exports. In OECD [Organization for Economic Cooperation and Development] countries, demand for African products has been limited. Agricultural protectionism and subsidies in industrialized countries have limited market access and reduced world market prices. The lack of necessary inputs has impeded expansion in the supply of products for export. Finally, in some potentially significant areas, African exports have remained insufficiently competitive."[3] The report goes on to show that in spite of new concessions on agricultural products in Lome IV, ACP countries had in the early 1990s a lower share of the EC market than they had in 1975.

Multilateral institutions such as the Lome Convention inadvertently perpetuate dependence rather than self-reliance, and they impose priorities that are not salient for Africa. When the convention started in 1975, it was praised as a welcome example of aid without strings. But the judgment was premature. Already by 1977 the Lome Convention began to reveal the inevitable conditionalities. By 1983–84 structural adjustment had become the dominant issue in the Lome Convention. "Policy dialogue" and policy reform are now firmly established as marks of sound economic management for ACP countries, decisive for sharing in the benefits of the Lome Convention. Under Lome IV, ECU1,150 million is reserved under the EDF for structural adjustment reform. As the political and economic integration of Europe progresses, the ACP countries increasingly face a monopoly power that pulls them ever more forcefully toward the European model of society.

Multilateral arrangements are expensive mainly because they are diversionary. The problems they address are highly selective, and the selectivity is defined largely by the perceptions and interests of the stronger party in the bargain, the donors. The Lome Convention does not really address the commodity issue despite its gestures in the direction of the stabilizing of commodity earnings. Lome IV provides ECU1,500 million under the EDF for Stabex and ECU480 million for Sysmin, quite insignificant sums for stabilizing commodity earnings of all the ACP countries over a period of five years. In any case, the fundamental problem is not stabilizing export earnings but being more productive, being more competitive, and breaking out of an international division of labor that confines Africa to commodity production.

3. World Bank and USAID (1991, p. 39).

Finally the Lome Convention does not address the debt problem. The EC's basic position has been that there is very little the community can do about the debt problem of ACP countries, on the ground that the debt issue is one of bilateral relations, that with only 2 percent of ACP countries' debts the EC is an insignificant creditor. In the spirit of this disclaimer, the EC does not offer any significant initiatives for dealing with the debt problem. Invariably, it offers only token measures: a slightly lower interest rate on EIB loans from the EIB's own funds, an increase in the grant components of EDF financing, offers of technical assistance for debt management, a willingness to discuss the ACP's debts, provided it is understood that the EC will not interfere with the prerogatives of the London and Paris Clubs to deal with their debtors.

The Debt Problem

Most leaders in Africa continue to assume that development is essentially a matter of making adjustments in the vertical relations between Africa and the wealthy nations of the North. In the name of development, African leaders have been preoccupied with finding access to northern markets and obtaining more loans on better terms, more foreign investment, better prices for African commodities, access to technology, technical assistance, debt cancellations, and net financial flows in favor of Africa. But these do not constitute a feasible development option.

The debt problem is not an aberration. It is inherent in the development strategies that Africa has been pursuing, in the location of Africa in the world economy, and in the prevailing international division of labor; its persistence and magnitude underline the limitations of present development strategies and the difficulties of overcoming them.

The Worsening Situation

The debt of developing countries was partly a product of the decade 1974-84, when the effective cartel strategy of the Organization of Petroleum Exporting Countries (OPEC) produced the great oil boom. Some of the surplus earned by OPEC members found its way to the industrialized market economies, whose banks began to have excess liquidity. Since the demand for capital had been dampened by the economic slack resulting from high energy costs, those economies began to encourage developing countries to borrow money to mop up the excess liquidity. In some cases, such as Nigeria, which was seen as having good prospects, credit was liberally extended.

African countries took advantage of the availability of credit, borrowed enthusiastically, and made poor investments with their easy credit. Between 1974 and 1982 the nominal dollar value of the debts of developing countries rose from $140 billion to $560 billion. In Africa the debt increased even more dramatically. By the end of 1984 Africa's external public and publicly guaranteed debt was about $145 billion, a sevenfold increase in indebtedness from 1974. In the same period real output fell by about 1 percent a year. By 1990 Africa's debt had leapt to $250 billion, a virtually unserviceable magnitude, given Africa's economic resources.

While Africa was getting deeper into debt, its inability to repay was increasing. According to the International Monetary Fund, the terms of trade of Sub-Saharan Africa was: -0.3 on the average for 1970-79; -3.3 in 1980; -4.5 in 1981 and 1982; 1.6 in 1983; 6.4 in 1984; -1.6 in 1985; -15.2 in 1986; 4.8 in 1987.[4] The export earnings of Sub-Saharan Africa, considerable in the period 1975 to 1980, declined sharply after a peak of $30 billion (excluding Nigeria) in 1980. They averaged only about $26 billion annually between 1980 and 1986. If Nigeria is included, the decline is more precipitate, from an average of $49 billion between 1979 and 1981 to only $35 billion for 1986-87.[5]

With mounting indebtedness, declining export earnings, and deteriorating terms of trade, new commercial lending became more difficult, and the prospects of economic recovery worsened. Africa's loans are characterized by stiff conditions that might be getting stiffer. The average interest rate on African debts is about 6 percent, which is very high considering the eligibility of many African countries for concessionality.[6] In the last decade many more African countries have been struggling to reschedule their loans in the context of the Paris Club, but they have not had the benefit of easy terms such as those of Mexico. The charges have usually been too high, the periods have been too short, and new capital has been very scarce.

Debt-servicing obligations in Africa have reached a point at which they are a major obstacle to economic growth. As table 4-2 indicates, the ratio of external debt to exports is so high that growth is all but impossible. The general statistics understate the hopeless situation of many African countries, some of whose debt ratios exceed 1,000. For instance, as of

4. IMF (1988, p. 181).
5. IMF (1988, p. 178).
6. IMF (1988, p. 184).

TABLE 4-2. *External Debt and Debt Service Ratios of Selected Indebted Developing Country Groups, 1980–87*
Percent

Item[a]	1980	1981	1982	1983	1984	1985	1986	1987
Ratio of year-end external debt to export[b]								
Sub-Saharan Africa[c]	147.9	184.3	218.5	231.5	227.7	271.7	296.8	325.1
Countries with recent debt-servicing problems[d]	152.0	186.5	240.3	253.8	244.1	265.4	304.6	298.7
Fifteen heavily indebted countries[e]	168.2	202.4	267.6	289.1	269.1	286.8	344.2	328.9
Ratio of year-end external debt to GDP[b]								
Sub-Saharan Africa[c]	38.6	43.1	49.3	51.8	54.9	61.4	61.6	69.0
Countries with recent debt-servicing problems[d]	33.7	39.3	43.6	46.4	47.0	48.6	49.2	48.7
Fifteen heavily indebted countries[e]	32.8	37.8	42.3	46.3	45.6	45.5	46.8	48.3
Ratio of debt service to exports								
Sub-Saharan Africa[c]	16.8	20.2	23.1	22.7	25.5	26.9	28.5	24.5
Countries with recent debt-servicing problems[d]	26.6	32.0	38.8	32.2	33.5	33.5	35.0	29.0
Fifteen heavily indebted countries[e]	29.4	38.8	48.9	39.3	39.5	39.2	43.2	35.9
Ratio of interest service to exports[f]								
Sub-Saharan Africa[c]	7.6	8.9	10.7	10.9	11.3	12.0	12.7	10.6
Countries with recent debt-servicing problems[d]	12.9	18.2	23.7	22.3	22.9	22.9	21.8	17.0
Fifteen heavily indebted countries[e]	15.9	22.6	30.6	29.1	29.1	28.6	28.0	21.8

SOURCES: IMF (1988, p. 182); IMF, *World Economic Outlook*, various years.
a. Exports include goods and services.
b. Excludes debt owed to the IMF.
c. Includes Nigeria.
d. Defined as capital-importing developing countries that incurred external payments arrears during 1985 or rescheduled their debt during 1984–86.
e. Includes two Sub-Saharan African countries: Nigeria and Ivory Coast.
f. Includes interest payments on total debt plus amortization payments on long-term debt only.

the end of 1987, the debt ratio for Guinea-Bissau was 1,500, for Somalia, 1,428.6, and for Sudan, 1,520.1.[7] Africa spent $23 billion on debt servicing in 1990. But this amount would have been much higher were it not for the fact that only 60 percent of the debt obligations due were serviced, while the rest were rescheduled.

What are the prospects for dealing with the debt burden in Africa? One way out of the problem would be increased export earnings that would create enough trade surplus to service debt and maintain growth. The difficulty here is that for most African countries the ratio of debts to exports is not decreasing but rising, in some cases, very steeply. For Sub-Saharan Africa as a whole, the ratio of debts to exports rose from 296.8 percent in 1986 to 334.6 percent in 1990.[8] These percentages reflect the low and negative growth rates in export volume and export earnings. The purchasing power of African exports has been falling substantially. Measured with 1980 as base year, it fell from an average of 76 percent in 1981–85 to 54 percent in 1986–90. It will be extremely difficult to reverse these tendencies enough for Africa to reduce its debt-export ratio substantially. Africa will need an export growth rate of about 10 percent to clear the interest on debts and have scope for a very modest growth, but such a performance is unlikely.

Data from the UN Conference on Trade and Development (UNCTAD) indicate that between 1986 and 1990, export volume grew at an annual rate of 2.5 percent. Worse still, Africa's export earnings fell in nominal terms from an annual average of $62.3 billion in 1981–85 to $54.8 billion in 1986–90.

Tentative Attempts to Solve the Problem

The debt burden of Africa is so great and the capacity to repay so limited that it is increasingly necessary to think not in terms of servicing but in terms of debt stock reduction and write-offs. The international development community has taken some steps in this direction. Just before the 1988 summit of the Group of Seven (G-7) in Toronto, President François Mitterrand announced that France was writing off one-third of the debt owed by the poorest countries. In April 1990 Italy canceled $1 billion ODA debt, some of which was owed by African countries. All in all, France has canceled roughly $2.4 billion owed by thirty-five African countries; and the United States has canceled $1.4 billion owed by twenty-

---

7. IMF (1988, p. 190).
8. IMF (1988, p. 182).

two African countries that have implemented structural adjustment programs.

What might be promising here is the apparent acceptance of the idea of debt cancellation. But the actual amounts canceled are small. According to World Bank estimates, between 1978 and 1990 donors canceled only $7.6 billion of debt, a virtually insignificant amount for a twelve-year period considering that, at Africa's current level of indebtedness, the yearly requirement for full servicing is roughly $40 billion. Debt forgiveness has had very little effect on debt-servicing burdens of Africa not only because the amounts being canceled are very small but also because the canceled debts are concessional debts associated with the ODA. The debt cancellations reduced the debt-service payments of African countries in 1990 by less than $100 million out of a total debt-service payment of $10 billion.

It is not likely that there will be a significantly higher level of debt forgiveness. For one thing, as the report of the UN secretary-general on UNPAAERD showed, "Africa's debt structure and debt-service payments have become concentrated and more inflexible, being tied to a rise in the share of multilateral financial institutions, most notably the World Bank and the IMF," whose debt is never forgiven and must be fully serviced."[9] Thus in 1989 all countries (except four) owing the multilateral agencies fully serviced their debts; 86 percent of the amount due was paid. Currently multilateral debt accounts for 21 percent of Africa's total debt, compared with 41 percent for official bilateral debt and 38 percent for private debt. The share of medium-term and long-term multilateral debt increased in Sub-Saharan Africa from 18.8 percent of the total debt in 1980 to 26.6 percent in 1990.[10]

Private credit is not as important in Africa as in other parts of the world. As of 1990 Sub-Saharan Africa owed only $30.6 billion, or 22 percent, of its total indebtedness. But private debts are a special problem in that private creditors do not appear to have strong reasons for cooperating in easing Africa's debt burden. On the whole, they have been adamant against write-offs and reduction of interest rates, and their rescheduling terms have been stringent. Commercial banks usually have no confidence that African economies will recover. Indeed, the arguments made by well-meaning people for debt relief for Africa, whether in terms of partial or total write-offs, a cut in interest rates, or long moratoriums, have inevitably focused on the vulnerability of African economies and therefore may have reinforced this lack of confidence. The doubts have not been helped by

9. UNCTAD (1991).
10. World Bank and USAID (1991, p. 44).

the political difficulties of implementing structural adjustment programs in Africa, or by the intense debate and increasing skepticism about the effectiveness of those programs.

The banks are quite naturally concerned with their interests in the context of their business strategies. For many of them, their goal is now to reduce their exposure in Africa. Those that have significant financial stakes, and many corporate clients in Africa do, will have some interest in debt management arrangements that will improve the liquidity of their African debtors. But those whose stakes are smaller are more inclined to cut loose and run; they are not likely to be interested in debt management operations, such as restructuring, even if it means that the actual value of their debt is depreciated. Even for the former group of commercial banks, their concern with debt management arrangements that will improve Africa's liquidity is weakened by the fact that what Africa owes them is relatively small.

Banks that want to lend new money are discouraged by the rising free-rider syndrome, that is, a state of affairs in which restructuring agreements allow creditors to collect the full interest on their outstanding loans without contributing new money or conditions to generate this interest payment. Because African debtors are so desperate for debt restructuring, commercial creditors are able to insist on restructuring agreements that have elements of the free-rider syndrome.

In recent years there has been less talk about cancellation and more emphasis on new approaches, at any rate new techniques of debt management that purportedly provide more flexibility in reconciling the interests of creditors and debtors. These have been characterized as the market-based menu approach. The elements of this approach include security and debt-conversion techniques such as exit instruments, debt-equity conversion, lending and relending facilities, and interest- and currency-switching options, as well as new money instruments such as interest capitalization, commodity-linked bonds, interest-retiring agreements, and new money bonds. For reasons that need not detain us here, many of these methods are not suitable for African conditions and are not likely to contribute much to debt relief or economic recovery. But some of them have considerable potential for reducing the debt burden of Africa if explored carefully in the context of a sound macroeconomic framework.

Two American plans for dealing with the debt crisis have generated a great deal of attention, the Baker plan and the Brady plan. But neither plan is a feasible strategy for dealing with the debt crisis in Africa. The

Brady plan, which is the more interesting because it appears to indicate the U.S. Treasury's implicit acceptance of partial debt write-off, has been more notable for the controversy surrounding it than for its effectiveness in dealing with the crisis. The controversy got so heated that a defensive Treasury began to quibble that it was offering not so much a plan as some ideas for discussion.

But that did not reduce the confusion and the controversy. Some objected that the proposal seemed more concerned with reducing the losses of commercial banks than in bringing relief to poor countries. The international financial institutions, especially the IMF, did not like the prospect of looking like guarantors of the debts of commercial banks. The suggestion implicit in the Brady plan that funds from the IMF and the World Bank might be used as a subsidy for commercial banks that discount their debts did not sit well with some of the contributors to those agencies. Great Britain, for one, made it clear that it did not accept the idea.

The Brady plan was the Group of Seven's idea of the way out of the debt crisis. It had been offered after the group had rejected a proposal for a North-South summit to discuss, among other things, the debt problem. Also rejected by the G-7 was a proposal for a debt moratorium, the setting up of an international fund for debt insurance, and a new multilateral lending institution proposed by Helmut Schmidt, then the West German chancellor. The rejection of these modest but useful proposals suggests that the Brady plan could not have been a really effective response to the debt crisis—even if it had succeeded on its own terms.

A serious attempt to deal with the problem would have had to take into consideration the impact of interest rates in the industrialized countries on the indebtedness of poor countries. For instance, a 1 percent rise of interest rates would increase indebtedness far more than all the Brady plan funds would cover. Even within the context of such a plan, the regional specificity of Africa is not considered, perhaps because of its small share of third world debts. Only Nigeria and Cameroon were clear candidates for benefiting from the reductions that might have arisen from the Brady plan.

There is no sign that Africa's creditors will cancel its debt on a large scale or grant the continent substantial relief. And there is no chance that Africa can pay its debts or even grow out of them, because the very reasons that call forth and sustain the debt also constrain economic growth. In any case, the debt burden of Africa, oppressive as it is, is not a fundamental problem but only a symptom. Even if all of Africa's debts were canceled, it would not make much difference as long as those conditions, such as inappropriate policies, corruption, disarticulated economies, and Africa's location in the international division of labor, remain.

Commodities

Commodities are a critical element in the relationship between Africa and the industrialized countries. African leaders believe that if Africa got good, stable prices for its commodities, its terms of trade and its debt problems might not exist or would be less burdensome. That is why they have been greatly concerned about adjusting this aspect of the relation of Africa and the North. They see commodity prices as an important element in a strategy of economic recovery and development.

In the present international division of labor, Africa is the quintessential primary producer. In 1965 primary products accounted for 92 percent of Africa's merchandise exports. Since then, the share of primary products in Sub-Saharan Africa's merchandise trade has hardly changed. For instance, in 1988 it was still 88 percent, despite all the years of effort to industrialize and diversify the productive and export base of African economies. African economies are not only commodity dependent, they are dependent in a very fragile way, as the export concentration ratio is very high.

Africa's dependence on primary commodities for its export earnings has become a major element of the crisis of underdevelopment in the light of trends in the prices of primary commodities and their implications for the terms of trade. Africa's share of the world market in commodities is declining, as are its terms of trade and purchasing power. These trends have been disastrous for the continent. Between 1980 and 1987 Africa lost fully 50 percent of the purchasing power of its export earnings. The future trends are not promising. It is estimated that by the year 2000 commodity prices will be about 25 percent below the level of 1980.

If one examines the factors behind these long-run trends, one sees that they are not likely to disappear. On the contrary, in the very long run, prospects may be gloomier still. The industrialized countries get better organized all the time for the defense of their common interests against the developing countries under a growing list of agencies, including the OECD, the G-7, the General Agreement on Tariffs and Trade (GATT), the Paris Club, and the London Club. One issue on which the industrialized countries have been singularly touchy in recent years is the price of primary commodities. They constantly worry about how a rise in commodity prices will add to their inflation rates, and they are ever ready to deal with any signs of a price surge in primary commodities. They are not necessarily against developing countries' getting more for their commodities; one presumes they would not mind an increase so much if it carried no threat of inflation, however small. But that is unlikely unless the rise in commodity prices is accompanied by a relative fall in wages in the industrialized countries. And that is indeed unlikely.

African commodity producers suffer from protectionism even in a world that is making a theology of market forces. A 1988 study by the Overseas Development Institute, *Commodity Prices: Investing in Decline?* has underlined this tendency. For instance, in Japan the prices paid to agricultural producers were on the average 2.5 times higher than world prices, in the EC countries 1.5 times higher, and in the United States 1.1 times higher. Because of protectionism, the EC countries became net exporters of grain. The EC, which imported 16 million tons of grain in 1970, exported 16 million tons in 1985.[11]

It would appear, however, that Africa's commodity problem has less to with the Machiavellian designs of the North than with objective forces, especially the changing structure of production occasioned by advances in science and technology. As mentioned, there has been a shift from material-based manufacturing such as shoemaking and tire manufacture to knowledge-based manufacturing industries such as computers; there has also been a shift from the production of goods to services. Because of these changes, the share of manufacturing in GDP has been decreasing gradually since 1965, and the share of services has been increasing.[12]

Changes in the technology of production are reducing the primary commodity content of manufactures. Thus it has been estimated that since 1900 the quantity of raw materials needed for a given unit of manufacture has been declining slowly but steadily at a rate of 1.25 percent a year compounded. The biotechnology revolution is threatening commodity producers, too. By techniques like tissue culture, tropical primary products or their equivalents can now be produced in laboratories in the North. Protein for animal feed may soon be produced from petroleum in European laboratories and factories and make the export of soybeans and cassava unnecessary. However, there is some chance that new possibilities for these commodities might open up. Also, as the Overseas Development

11. Overseas Development Institute (1988).
12. Drucker (1986).

Institute reports, research is under way in Europe for the production of such commodities as cocoa butter and pyrethrum. It is telling that all the changes discussed here are irreversible.

The preoccupation of African leaders and the international development community with the fluctuations of commodity prices and the worsening of the terms of trade for commodity producers is understandable. It is indeed highly desirable that Africa earn more for its commodities and that commodity prices be more stable. Certainly much can said for retaining and, if possible, increasing market shares, for increasing productivity and export intensity in commodities.

But Africa must look beyond these concerns, for they are not really the solution and the problems they raise are considerable. For instance, as cocoa producers in West Africa have discovered, increased productivity across the board may leave primary producers poorer as they compete among themselves and force down world commodity prices. Africa needs to be productive and competitive and to diversify and strive for industrialization instead of being fixated on commodity prices.

The commodity problem is real. But it is poorly conceived and exaggerated. It is the symptom of the more fundamental failures in development strategies that have hindered productivity, competitiveness, diversification, and industrialization. Higher commodity prices would not contribute much to the resolution of the African crisis, whose causes lie in the limitation of the broader policy framework and in a political context that is detrimental to development.

Conclusion: Marginalization and Self-Reliance

African leaders and the international development community alike are now less interested in grand strategies of development. The emphasis has shifted to pragmatism, to such policy instruments and options as encouraging foreign investment, eliminating or reducing the debt burden, improving the terms of trade, and realizing greater production, export intensity, and better prices for commodities. Those options suggest that development can be achieved by relatively modest adjustments on the vertical relationship between Africa and the North. However, doing so is not an appropriate policy option. As discussed, the necessary adjustments are problematic. But even if they were not so problematic, this approach would still fail. To understand why, one must put considerations on Africa and the global economy in the context of the discourse on the marginalization of Africa. For only in that context can one clearly see the economic and political constraints on the strategy of development by adjustment of the vertical relations between Africa and the North and also the reasons why the African crisis is primarily political rather than economic.

Marginalization and Its Genesis

What is the discourse on the marginalization of Africa saying? What exactly does the marginalization of Africa mean? What is being said is quite clear and simple. The concern is mainly (but not exclusively) with economic marginalization, with the economic regression of Africa relative to other regions of the world and the diminishing importance and relevance of Africa to the global economy, particularly to the industrialized countries. The statistics of Africa's role in the global economy make the point well enough. Africa's share of exports in world trade, which was only 2.4 percent in 1970, was down to 1.4 percent by 1990. Even its share of non-oil primary commodities fell from 7 percent to less than 4 percent in the same period.[13] That is why Africa was deservedly voiceless at the GATT negotiations and quite predictably came out worse than any other region. A 1993 study for the World Bank and the OECD Development Center estimates that, on account of the GATT agreement, the world will be at least $213 billion richer a year by 2002, whereas Sub-Saharan Africa will be $2.6 billion a year poorer.[14]

Like every other key indicator, net financial flows to Africa have been diminishing steadily. Significantly, the decline continued even after 1986, the year that the world community set out to reverse such trends by launching UNPAAERD. Net financial resource flow to Africa was $15.8 billion in 1985, $22.2 billion in 1990, and $18.4 billion in 1992. But at 1985 constant dollars and if allowance is made for profit, interest, and capital repayment, net financial transfers to Africa in real terms declined to $10.4 billion in 1990 and $5.3 billion in 1992. Overseas development assistance fell from $19.7 billion in 1990 to $18.3 billion in 1991 and $12.1 billion in 1992.

This trend holds for bilateral relations between most industrialized countries and Africa. Perhaps the United States is a good example, since it is an important country that was not a colonial power. U.S. interest in

13. Serageldin (1993, p. 95).
14. Goldin, Knudsen, and van der Mensbrugghe (1993).

Africa began and peaked in 1958-62, driven by the Kennedy administration's concern about a communist presence starting from Egypt and spreading to the rest of Africa. In this period U.S. aid to Africa rose from $110 million to $519 million and Africa's share of U.S. aid increased from 2 percent to 8 percent.[15] But when the fear turned out to be exaggerated, U.S. interest waned. In the decade 1963-73 U.S aid to Africa declined steadily, from $519 million in 1963 to $286 million in 1973.[16] Africa accounted for 6.0 percent of U.S. imports in 1975, 4.1 percent in 1983, and roughly 2.0 percent in 1988. Africa's share of U.S. exports was 3.0 percent in 1970, 2.2 percent in 1983, and only 1.2 percent in 1988. In 1988 Sub-Saharan Africa accounted for only 1 percent of total U.S. investment in developing countries, and this investment was concentrated in the oil-producing countries of Nigeria, Angola, Cameroon, and Gabon.[17] By 1990 Africa got only 0.46 percent of U.S. investment. Insignificant as this percent is, it is still declining. The economic marginality of Africa to the United States is now also being reflected in other spheres. For instance, the staffs of the Bureau of African Affairs of the State Department and the Africa Desk of the USAID are being decreased. The USAID has also been reducing its missions in Africa.[18]

How can one account for the problem of marginalization? Perhaps it is not necessary to do so, because the problem is more apparent than real. What is popularly called the problem of marginalization is essentially a restatement of the perennial problem of underdevelopment. Marginalization is in reality the dynamics of underdevelopment, the development of underdevelopment by the agents of development. According to the World Bank, the average annual growth rate of GNP per capita for Africa was 1.3 percent between 1980 and 1990 and − 0.6 percent in 1991.[19] Average agricultural (weighted) growth rate for 1970 to 1980 in Africa was 1.5 percent. With population growth rate averaging above 3 percent, Africa has became food dependent and prone to chronic malnutrition. Industrial value added has been virtually stagnant. The 1989 long-term perspective study by the World Bank, *Sub-Saharan Africa: From Crisis to Sustainable Growth*, set a target of 5 percent value added for 1990 and then 7 percent to 8 percent for subsequent years.[20] But Africa managed only 2.1 percent

15. Clough (1992, p. 7).
16. Clough (1992, p. 9).
17. Michaels (1992-93, p. 95).
18. Michaels (1992-93, p. 94).
19. World Bank (1993a, p. 199).
20. World Bank (1989b, p. 4).

in 1990 and 2.9 percent in 1991, and there seems to be no chance of substantial improvement in the short to medium term.[21] Indicators such as industrial value added could not improve with the weak performance in capital formation, a crucial statistic.

The World Bank study also targeted a rate of 25 percent of GDP for gross domestic investment for Sub-Saharan Africa in the 1990s. But between 1989 and 1991, the rates declined from 21.9 percent to 16.0 percent.[22] With a very low rate of return on investment and strong competition from Asia, the former Soviet-bloc countries, and Latin America, Africa's ability to attract foreign direct investment, already very poor, will not improve and might get worse. Foreign direct investment in Sub-Saharan Africa, small even at its peak of $2,303 million in 1989, was only $570 million in 1990 (Indonesia alone got $964 million in the same year) and $669 million in 1991.[23] The state of financial resource flows to Africa can be seen from the fact that even the World Bank group, the agents of African development, have been recording negative transfers since the late 1980s. The terms of trade are against Africa, to the detriment of its growth potential. The average index fell by about 23 percent between 1985 and 1987 and then hovered around the same level until 1991, when it fell again by 8.9 percent.[24]

In these circumstances Africa has become heavily indebted. Sub-Saharan Africa's debt as a percentage of GNP was 28.6 percent in 1980 and 107.9 percent in 1991. As a percentage of total exports it was 96.6 percent in 1980 and 329.4 percent in 1991. Debt service as a percentage of exports was 10.9 percent in 1980 and 20.8 percent in 1981.[25] It looks as though Africa can neither pay its debts nor grow out of them.

For the most part, Africa has been stagnating or regressing economically. It has therefore become unattractive to foreign investors, unable to import or export much and so a virtual nonentity in world trade, and increasingly unable to elicit the interest of other regions. The decline is not just a cause of marginality; it is also the process of marginalization. The discourse on marginalization is really about the deepening crisis of underdevelopment.

21. Global Coalition for Africa (1992, p. 6).
22. Global Coalition for Africa (1992, p. 36).
23. Global Coalition for Africa (1992, p. 41).
24. Global Coalition for Africa (1992, p. 36).
25. World Bank (1993e, p. 285). The 1980 figures cited here exclude Nigeria and therefore differ from those in table 4-2. If Nigeria were included here, the percentages would be much larger.

Agents of Marginalization

A notable weakness of the marginalization discourse is that it does not address the real problem. Who is decrying marginalization? Who or what is getting marginalized? By what? In what regard? Strangely enough, the discourse about the fate of Africa focuses on non-Africans. It orchestrates concerns about non-Africans not taking enough interest in Africa, not doing enough with it or for it, not giving it consideration. It worries about external social forces being allowed to complicate or even defeat Africa's bid to escape from underdevelopment. And it encourages non-Africans to pay more benevolent attention to Africa.

Somehow the discourse manages to forget that it is natural and appropriate that Africa should be marginal to non-Africans, just as it should be primary to Africans. Worse still, it represents the development of Africa as being not so much what Africans do as what is done by outsiders about Africa. Development is strategized in such a way that those who have the most interest in development, those who should be its means and ends— the Africans themselves—are marginalized. As a result, real development becomes impossible. In effect, the agents of development in Africa, namely, the African elites and the international development community, engendered this exogenous development strategy.

The African elites marginalized the African role in the development of Africa by their politics. When the elites succeeded the colonial regime, they chose to inherit the colonial system rather than transform it in accordance with the democratic aspirations of the nationalist movement. Invariably, the elites fell out with their followers and became repressive. Repression bred more hostility, inviting more repression, in a continuing spiral. As a result, reactionary monolithism has dominated Africa in the form of single-party regimes and military rule. Military rule in Africa reflects a reality that was already fully formed. It was not the military that caused military rule in Africa by intervening in politics; it was the character of politics that engendered military rule. By degenerating into warfare, politics propelled the specialists of violence to the lead role.

Beset by a multitude of hostile forces that their betrayal of the nationalist movement and their political repression had created, the African elites developed a siege mentality. They became so absorbed in the struggle for survival that they could not pay much attention to anything else, especially development. More often than not, the things that the elites did to hang on to power became impediments to development. For example, they manipulated ethnic and communal loyalties to elicit loyalty and establish common cause with some communities. In doing so, they divided into hostile camps not only the elites but also the wider society and transformed ethnicity into a violent and highly destructive force in many countries, including Togo, Congo, Rwanda, Kenya, Liberia, Angola, Uganda, Ethiopia, Burundi, Mauritania, Zaire, Nigeria, and Sudan. In trying to consolidate their power and to prevent rivals and opponents from having access to power, they used state power to control the economy and to appropriate wealth. This political strategy created an unproductive state capitalism in which surplus was accumulated and distributed with state power, and the law of value could not take root. The system has spawned administrative controls and regulations whose power of enforcement is used corruptly.

Entrepreneurship has been discouraged. Economic success is dependent on state power or state patronage. For anyone outside the dominant faction of the political elites, it was generally futile to harbor hopes of becoming wealthy by entrepreneurial activity or even to take personal safety for granted. So these people directed their energy to seeking the inside track on power. For those who were part of the ruling faction, entrepreneurial activity became unnecessary, since wealth could be accumulated faster and with less risk by using state power. So entrepreneurship was blocked at both ends.

A predatory state and Hobbesian politics have ruined the prospects of development by spreading alienation, resentment, inefficiency, and corruption. Politically disenfranchised and set upon by state violence, the people are no longer available for supporting the state or its development project. Some of them have retreated to ethnic or communal identity and local concerns. Political repression has forced highly educated and talented people to become political or economic refugees in other countries, their talents lost to the cause of national development.

Having marginalized development as well as the vital agents of development, African leaders have been reduced to making token gestures to development while attempting to shift the responsibility for it to foreign patrons. Although they talked about the fragility of political independence and the need to buttress it by means of self-reliant development, they eagerly embraced economic dependence and allowed outsiders to conceptualize and manage development, thus marginalizing even their own role in development. That is the background to the exogenous development and the economic regression that is all too apparent in Africa today.

With the initiative for development conceded in this manner, development came to be regarded not so much as what Africans do as what others might do for Africa. Programmatically it was regarded as incremental adjustments in the vertical relation between Africa and the industrialized countries in Africa's favor: more aid on more lenient terms, more access for African goods in Western markets and on better terms, more transfer of technology, more investment, and more debt forgiveness.

The Benefits of Marginalization

Perhaps marginalization, so often decried, is what Africa needs right now. For one thing, it will help the evolution of an endogenous development agenda, an agenda that expresses the aspirations of the people and can therefore elicit their support. Because of exogeneity, and its contradictions, Africa does not even at this late stage have a development agenda. As noted, what Africa has is a confusion of agendas, reflecting the demonstrated failure of an exogenous agenda that its promoters do not acknowledge and the unfulfilled promise of an endogenous agenda that African leaders are too dependent and too diffident to push through.

The marginalization of Africa in the world economy could be useful in another important sense. Insofar as it leaves the development of Africa to Africans, it offers a chance of breaking out of another major development trap—the dissociation of development strategy from social experience. This problem arises from the values and social situation of the external agents and patrons of development. The external agents who are "developing" Africa inevitably see development as the reproduction of their own society, achievable by their own tutelage and the gradual transfer of relevant values from their society to Africa. This view underlies the familiar notion of development as an adjustment of the vertical relationship between Africa and the industrialized countries, by transferring resources downward.

When a people must be developed not by themselves but by others, development becomes a benevolence that is largely insensitive to social needs. In Africa, one might say, what currently prevails is development against the people—not of them or for them. The African variety of structural adjustment, well-meaning as it might be or even "necessary," is an excellent example of this odd phenomenon. In the name of economic growth, real incomes are reduced by as much as 40 percent or more overnight. The prices of social services and staples are raised enormously, and inflation rates soar. These are the kinds of magnitudes of austerity that have earned the IMF the title of mad doctor. They break down social consensus, cause violent conflict, anxiety and deep despair, and sometimes premature death on a large scale, especially among children. These grim notions of policy reform can be inflicted only by people who do not belong to the adjusting society or by those who are immune to the impact of the reform.

However, the scientific validity or long-run effects of structural adjustment may be rationalized, and whatever the good intentions of its managers, the undeniable fact is that these managers cannot be held to account. Social needs cannot be externally defined. Only endogenous development can bring development strategy into harmony with social needs.

Foreign development agents do not see the people as agents of development or as the essential energy that must fuel it, as a source of ideas of how to proceed, or even as a constituency to which the agents are accountable. With few exceptions, they do not take seriously the idea of the people developing themselves. They also have political interests that are unlikely to be served by making development an open-ended democratic process, determined by the will of the people, drawing on their energy, and serving their interest.

Neither do most African leaders act as if they believe in the need for their people to be the engine of development. They assume that what development requires is known and clear: their own leadership and the passive acquiescence of the masses. Indeed, that was the ideological basis of the single-party regimes, as well as military rule, and the rationale for criminalizing dissent in Africa's interregnum of political authoritarianism. But having marginalized the people, this development paradigm cannot draw on their support, and it cannot even be put into effect. Leaders are obliged to look outside for aid, investment, and technical assistance rather than tap the energy of the people. So the strategy that was originally an effect of the alienation and marginalization of the people becomes also its cause. There is no development in alienation.

Development can only be related to and driven by social will in the context of democracy. It is only in this context that the people can be the means and the end of development. Without democracy, the advantages of demarginalizing Africans in the development process and giving them control cannot be realized. With minor exceptions, African elites have placed great obstacles in the way of development by their antipathy to democracy.

The international development community has compounded these obstacles in its confusion over the merits of exogeneity and the relationship between democracy and the market. It assumes that it is promoting democracy and development simultaneously by supporting policy reform and political conditionality. To do so depends on a prior assumption, namely, that the liberation of market forces is *never* contradictory to democratization even in the short run. But this is mistaken; that relationship is mediated in very complex ways by historical conjunctures and permutations of sequences of democratization and market reform and any number of other salient intervening variables.

The African Experience

Without going into these complexities, I want to make a few general comments to show how, proceeding from their abstract assumptions about the harmony of market reform and democracy and development, the international development community has in fact been subverting democracy and development. It has not taken full account of two concrete particulars: exogeneity and the special character and content of policy reform in Africa.

The African experience shows that exogeneity defeats democracy, whatever the intentions of the developmental and economic policies associated with it. External development agents, who are presumably democrats, have felt constrained to give market reform priority over democracy. The most important issue of public policy, namely, structural adjustment programs (SAPs), is not subject to democratic choice, because the agents distrust the people's ability to chose correctly on an issue in which "the right choice" is absolutely clear. At the same time, SAPs are so draconian that they are assumed to require imposition.

Zambia's experience shows how these assumptions play out. Despite its breezy confidence, the development community is failing to reconcile its support of democracy with its support of SAPs. In effect, what has emerged is the following accommodation. The development community supports the African regime and its democratization on the understanding that it is disempowered, so it cannot choose against the market. Unable to go anywhere except with the SAPs, the government then proceeds to implement them, not by democratic sanction but by disempowering the people in turn and imposing the programs.

When the Kaunda government broke with the IMF in May 1987, and adopted a home-grown reform program, the New Economic Reform Program, the Zambia Congress of Trade Unions (ZCTU) supported the move "in the national interest." Also, when the government went back to the IMF in September 1989 after the failure of the program, the ZCTU remained consistent and opposed that action. However, in 1990 ZCTU decided to support the Movement for Multiparty Democracy (MMD), a political formation dominated by business people and commercial farmers that was in favor of policy reform. With the help of ZCTU, the MMD came to power on October 31, 1991, in a landslide victory, capturing 125 out of the 150 seats in parliament.

The victory was a mandate for democracy. But it was also a mandate for reform. And the democratization mandate succumbed. After the victory of Frederick Chiluba and the MMD, the Western powers poured aid into Zambia. As was to be expected, the aid was contingent on Zambia's embracing reform unequivocally, an easy conditionality because the MMD's internal financiers, the powerful Zambian business lobby called the G-7 Club was in favor of reform. So Chiluba embarked on a harsh, ambitious project of reform, which included astronomical inflation rates (fueled by the 500 percent increase in the price of maize meal) and the scaling down of social services.

The labor movement broke with the MMD government, denouncing the harshness of the reform program. The new president of the ZCTU, Fackson Shamenda, has complained that the MMD and the government are now captive to business interests. The unofficial labor strikes that were characteristic of the turbulent last years of the Kaunda regime have started again. Under pressure, Chiluba has become increasingly authoritarian; for instance, he dismissed four senior ministers, including the minister of finance, and belligerently refused to give an explanation. On March 8, 1993, he declared a state of emergency and gave himself extraordinary powers on the pretext of a plot to overthrow his government, the so-called Zero Option Plan.

President Chiluba, the symbol of the democratic revolution, became a means of disempowerment. With the support of the business and international community, his government subverted the democratic side of his dual mandate while pressing the other, policy reform, against the opposition of mass organizations. Though increasingly alienated and distressed, the people of Zambia have no place to turn; the Kaunda regime was so discredited and the victory of MMD was so commanding that there is currently no credible alternative.

However, Chiluba's winning coalition is in disarray. In August 1993, nine members of parliament resigned from the MMD, citing corruption and poor leadership, and declared their intention to form a new party to challenge Chiluba and the MMD in the election of 1996. Significantly, these were people who were crucial for the victory of the MMD in 1991. The president's biggest problem now appears to be the widespread belief that he is governed by Western donors, whose agenda has become dominant in Zambian public policy. He is perceived to have been forced by the West into giving the highest priority to fighting drug trafficking, a perception strengthened by his dismissal of Boniface Kwawimbe, his health minister, and Dean Mung' OMB, a deputy minister in the presidency. Seeing no alternative for now, Zambians are expressing themselves in the perfect metaphor of political disempowerment, apathy. In the local government elections of December 1992, fewer than 20 percent of the registered voters bothered to participate.

The experience of Zambia can be expected to occur repeatedly with minor variations, for exogeneity is incompatible with accountability—and that is only one of its patent irrationalities. There is no accountability in exogenous development because there is no way of holding the foreign managers of the economy responsible for the policies they initiate. They do not seek or need a democratic mandate from their client states. And yet their power is decisive. The World Bank and the IMF, in particular, have become the dominant power over economic management in Africa, by virtue of the resources they control, their monopoly of information, and their aura of scientific authority and by being the gateway to northern support. By all indications, the Bretton Woods institutions have unfortunately come to symbolize power without responsibility, rather like the failed national leadership.

With its principal players dissociated from the culture, the social needs, and the social will of the people supposedly being developed, exogeneity is singularly irrational. One cannot do social engineering successfully and without trauma by focusing on what ought to be, while refusing to take society as it is. Exogenous development implicitly assumes that development is politically neutral, an assumption clearly reflected in the tendency to place the most important decisions of public policy beyond politics and to find it appropriate to exercise power without responsibility. Exogeneity is also irrational in failing to recognize or in ignoring the interface of the economic and political markets. Only the economic market counts, not the political market that moderates it and ensures that its blind forces do not annul all collective purpose even as they confer the benefit of efficiency and productivity. Finally, exogeneity is irrational in the contradiction between its manifest and latent functions; the one develops for the people, the other against the people. It renders the political market inoperable and irrelevant.

To conclude, if Africa is marginal to the rest of the world, that is as it should be. The problem is not, as is often imagined, Africa's marginality to the rest of the world but the marginalization of Africans in the development of Africa. This is precisely why the development project in Africa cannot get started. Development is something that people do by themselves and for themselves, or it does not happen. The people of Africa will have to empower themselves to repossess their own development, a formidable task. Only a successful struggle for repossession will finally remove the obstacles that have until now grounded the development project.

5

The Residual Option

In this final chapter, I want to outline what the appropriate development paradigm for Africa might look like, taking account of present realities in Africa and the global environment at large. First I review the nature of the paradigm, I then examine its political presuppositions, and finally I consider its development strategy.

The Nature of the Paradigm

As an approach to development, this paradigm may be characterized as the residual option, to suggest what is likely to remain after separating out the confusions, irrelevances, frills, and distortions that stand in the way of strategizing development in Africa. What is left after this sorting-out process is the energy of ordinary people.

To avoid misunderstanding, it should be emphasized that what I offer here is the sketch of a paradigm, not a blueprint or an action plan. I do not go into the particulars of industrial and agricultural policies, tariff regimes, demand and supply management, or the methods for raising investment and saving ratios, labor productivity, export earnings, and the like. The paradigm will be necessarily formal and abstract.

A paradigm in this context can be only about the logic, the values, the principles, and the general path of movement, a theoretical structure of experience whose practical operation will vary depending on the historical circumstances of each country. To be sure, some concrete details will be needed for clarity. However, the paradigm cannot rest on the validity of such "facts"; its validity depends initially on its logic, its principles, and its grasp and articulation of the problem. This is not to deny that its ultimate vindication depends on the success or failure of those who practice it; but that is another matter.

It is important to remember that the logic, principles, and values of the paradigm are neither arbitrary constructs nor abstractions; they are derived from, indeed determined by, the problem. A paradigm is a manner of proceeding in regard to a problem, a possible solution. Therefore its constitution as well as its relevance depends crucially on the nature of the problem.

It is extremely important to bear this obvious but often neglected point in mind, because one of the difficulties of the development literature in Africa is the relation of problem and solution. Often the problem is unclear, and if so, it cannot have a solution. Scholars and agents of development tend to focus on ideologically derived answers to the problem of development that bear no relation to the nature of the problem. Their concern is not so much to solve a problem on its own terms as to realize an image of the world.

It is because of this bias that in the preceding chapters I have articulated what the problem is, what it is not, and what a particular understanding of an aspect of the problem entails. In this sense those chapters are an important part of the paradigm, if not the most important part, for they determine its character: its logic, its values, its principles, and the way in which they relate.

The basic assumptions of the paradigm are as follows:

—Development is not economic growth even though economic growth in large measure determines its possibility. A development paradigm cannot therefore be judged merely by its conduciveness to economic growth, although this criterion of judgment is not irrelevant to its validity.

—Development is not a project but a process.

—Development is the process by which people create and recreate themselves and their life circumstances to realize higher levels of civilization in accordance with their own choices and values.

—Development is something that people must do for themselves, although it can be facilitated by the help of others. If people are the end of development, as is the case, they are also necessarily its agent and its means.

—Africa and the global environment are to be taken as they are and not as they ought to be. What the paradigm contributes is some idea of what they can be.

These assumptions are largely the prevailing conventional wisdom of the development community. The only thing new here is that I take them seriously and apply them systematically, allowing them to color and shape every aspect of development. As will be seen, applying these assumptions systematically results in a markedly different way of approaching development from that prevailing today.

The difficulties of changing to a different way of seeing and doing things from those with which everyone is familiar are notorious. They are all the more so in the field of development, where the prevailing paradigm is so well established, so apparently plausible, and so embedded and legitimized in the existing structuration of power that the very idea of a possible alternative seems frivolous and utopian.

The Politics of the Development Paradigm

I want to begin by specifying the political context of the development paradigm. As has been seen, development strategies are not made and implemented in a political vacuum, especially since development is a collective enterprise. Every development strategy is always contextualized in a particular state, social structure, culture, and meaning. It implies a structure of politics, but it also influences political interactions, practices, and outcomes.

By the assumptions of the paradigm African countries can develop only in the context of democratic politics. Considerable confusion exists among scholars of development over the relationship between development and democracy. Some say there is no necessary relation between democracy and development. Some argue that democracy is detrimental to development; others think it is conducive to it. And some think the matter is one of sequencing. By all indications this confusion arises from scholars' not taking the assumptions, the conventional wisdom, seriously. Once that is done, the confusion disappears; there may be errors but not confusion.

The prevailing development ideology, like the paradigm, sees the people as the end of development. In practice, however, they are only nominally so. That is not surprising, since people cannot be the end of development unless they are already its agents and its means, a condition that has never been true in Africa. If the people are the agents of development—that is, those with the responsibility to decide what development is, what values it is to maximize, and the methods for realizing it—they must also have the prerogative of making public policy at all levels. They must not merely participate in the conventional sense of the word; they must be the ones who decide on how to proceed with social transformation. To be sure, up to a point it is possible for the people to be the means of development without the need for a democratic political system:

the people can be coerced or manipulated to give their resources to promote their leaders' notion of development. However, this process of enlisting the people's resources is oppressive and exploitative rather than emancipatory, and a process that is not emancipatory cannot be conducive to development. An oppressive and exploitative way of seeking development is a contradiction in terms. That leaves the option of the people making themselves the means of development, and this option requires political democracy.

Finally, if people are the end of development, then their well-being is the supreme law of development. But the well-being of the people will only be the supreme law of development if they have some decisionmaking power. It is possible of course that someone can exercise public decisionmaking power to the benefit of others. But the only one way to ensure that social transformation is not dissociated from the well-being of the people is to institute democracy.

In insisting on the necessity of political democracy, one should recognize that for the development community democracy in development is highly problematic and possibly undesirable. Some think that democracy tends to complicate the task of development or that it may be detrimental to development. No doubt the world as a whole and the development community in particular has been very impressed by what the newly industrializing countries (NICs)—notably, Thailand, Taiwan, South Korea, and Singapore—have achieved under authoritarian rule. The dramatic performance of China in the last fifteen years has reinforced this view. Although no one is saying that countries seeking development should embrace authoritarianism, some believe that the new emphasis on democracy in Africa is misguided and may well be detrimental. Sometimes the discussion of the success of the East Asian countries hints at the need for a benign, efficient dictatorship with the "appropriate" macroeconomic framework.

There are many difficulties, some dilemmas, and not a little confusion in this debate, and some clarification is in order. To begin with, most people conflate development and economic growth. When they cite the impressive achievements of authoritarian countries such as South Korea in development, the content they give to development is usually economic growth. What I am interested in is development, and for present purposes the possible relation of political authoritarianism to development. A case for authoritarianism's being positively correlated to development does not really arise, because democracy is part of the very meaning of political development.

Still, it should be said that the authoritarianism of the East Asian economic growth is a complicated fact. As the World Bank study *The East Asian Miracle* indicates, the authoritarianism of the NICs in East Asia has certain "redeeming features"[1]—features that are usually associated with a democratic polity but that may also occur in a more rudimentary form in nondemocratic polities. These include accountability, predictability, the rule of law, and competition. In each of these countries a disciplined political class with a well-articulated national project of development achieved some element of accountability by taking its obligations to the nation seriously; it was able to achieve some predictability—lawful rule by its own internal discipline and by its understanding of the importance of predictability as a desirable business environment—as well as to achieve competition in certain stipulated spheres. Labeling the NICs autocratic is not inaccurate, but it conceals those features that signal the existence of some critical, though imperfect, democratic values. Political authoritarianism needs to be differentiated. The authoritarianism of the NICs of East Asia is entirely different from that of Africa, which tends to lack these rudimentary democratic values, to the detriment of economic growth.

If it is granted that these features played an important role in economic growth in the NICs of East Asia, these countries, far from refuting the usefulness of democracy to economic growth, give it some weak support. One might then argue that if authoritarian regimes are able to mimic some democratic values and use them effectively to achieve rapid economic growth, there is no need to put so much energy into clamoring for democracy. That would be a mistake, however. The existence of these limited democratic values in authoritarian regimes is fortuitous; it depends on the character and the will of the dominant faction of the political class. If these values are so necessary, their existence should not be merely fortuitous; it should be objective and guaranteed. But only in the context of a mature democracy can values such as the rule of law, accountability, transparency, and competitiveness be fully operational as well as guaranteed.

It is important to avoid thinking of Africa by making analogies and easy comparisons with the experiences of others, especially the NICs of East Asia. Political authoritarianism has its own specificity, which markedly affects its consequences. While in East Asia autocratic states are well established and in control, in most African countries there is really no state, liberal or autocratic. What exists is a public force that should be

1. World Bank (1993b).

the state but that is only nominally so because it is essentially privatized. Being privatized, the so-called state is not able to rise above the struggles and conflicts of contending social groups. It becomes itself a contested terrain where contending parties vie for the appropriation of resources, including the power of the state. All this spells an unusually intense political competition, in which the stakes are so high that the situation is essentially lawless; politics is basically warfare, or at best an anarchy of dedicated self seeking.

In most of Sub-Saharan Africa, unlike East Asia, the state not only is very rudimentary, if it can be said to exist at all, but was also displaced. It was displaced by colonialism, which in the course of its violent assault on indigenous society directed loyalties to primary groups, and also by the state-building project of the post-independence era, which was almost as coercive as the colonial state-building project and had roughly the same effect.

In Africa political authoritarianism prevents the crystallization of the state or even of a political class. Rather, it tends to constitute a plurality of "informal" primary groups that are largely the repository of loyalties. It unleashes powerful centrifugal forces that render the polity incoherent and unable to establish a common purpose, including a development project, and to pursue it effectively. In short, political authoritarianism is an important reason why the development project in Africa has not been able to take off.

The Feasibility of Democracy in Africa

It is not enough to settle the question of the desirability or even the necessity of democracy in Africa. How about its feasibility? In the context of my concern here with development, that is the critical question.

But before addressing this question, it is necessary to deal with a preliminary question: what is democracy? And, in particular, what is the kind of democracy whose feasibility is at issue in Africa? About this question there is also much arbitrariness and confusion. But once again, by taking the familiar assumptions of development practice seriously, the confusion can be dispelled. On these assumptions Africa requires somewhat more than the crude variety of liberal democracy that is being foisted on it, and even more than the impoverished liberal democracy that prevails in the industrialized countries.

The North's Attitude to Democracy in Africa

Even at its best, liberal democracy is inimical to the idea of the people having effective decisionmaking power. The essence of liberal democracy is precisely the abolition of popular power and the replacement of popular sovereignty with the rule of law. As it evolved, liberal democracy got less democratic as its democratic elements, such as the consent of the governed, the accountability of power to the governed, and popular participation, came under pressure from political elites all over the world as well as from mainstream social science, which seemed even more suspicious of democracy than political elites. On the pretext of clarifying the meaning of democracy, Western social science has constantly redefined it, to the detriment of its democratic values.

To illustrate, the group theory of politics evades the meaning of democracy and pushes the notion that the essence of democracy is the dynamics of group competition, which prevents the monopolization of power and allows the accommodation of the broad concerns of many groups. According to the interest group theory of democracy, the citizen is no longer a real or potential lawmaker, a participant in sovereignty, but only a supplicant for favorable policy results in accord with articulated interests. For the protective theory of democracy, the democratic polity is one in which the citizen is protected against the state, especially by virtue of a vibrant civil society. Sovereignty disappears as does participation as people settle for protection. In several important books political apathy has been praised for being conducive to political stability or for being a mark of satisfaction with the rulers.[2] More recently, in the hurry to globalize democracy in the wake of the cold war, democracy has been reduced to the crude simplicity of multiparty elections to the benefit of some of the world's most notorious autocrats, such as Daniel arap Moi of Kenya and Paul Biya of Cameroon, who are now able to parade democratic credentials without reforming their repressive regimes.[3]

For Africa, the concern of northern countries in promoting even this crude version of democracy is some progress. Through decades of involvement in Africa, the North's attitude had been that democracy is not for Africa. That attitude was an important component of the ideology of colonization, which held that Africans were unfit to govern themselves, that they needed the civilization of colonial tutelage as their one hope of eventually achieving self-determination and development.

2. See, for example, Almond and Verba (1963, 1980); Polsby (1963).
3. Ake (1991).

Even in the era of political independence in Africa, the North remained indifferent to issues of democracy on the continent, alienated by the nationalist onslaught on its presumptions and concerned that self-government, which Africans had so "hastily" demanded, would fail. Northern governments were happy to cooperate with the newly independent African governments in a "partnership in development"; they gave indulgent support to authoritarian African regimes in order to maintain influence and to protect their interests. This support was all too easily given because the authoritarian tendencies of the postcolonial era only confirmed the North's prejudices against the political maturity of Africa. In their quest for allies in the cold war, the great powers ignored considerations of human rights in Africa and sought clients wherever they could. All this crystallized opinion against democracy in Africa.

The prejudice was so strong that the question of democracy in Africa was hardly ever raised. From time to time—for instance, during the Carter administration in the United States—human rights became an issue, but never democracy. On the rare occasions when democracy was discussed, it was mainly to raise doubts about its feasibility.

From the early 1990s, issues of democratization and human rights began to dominate the North's interest in Africa, the result largely of the "capitalist" revolution in eastern Europe and the winding down of the cold war. The Soviet empire was, in the eyes of the West, the antithesis of democracy. The spectacle of the long, dramatic, and largely successful democratic struggles that took place after the breakup of the empire convinced the West that liberal democracy was feasible everywhere, and western nations began to be sensitive to democracy's possibilities even in Africa.

But Africa is so marginal now that it is difficult for non-Africans to bring themselves to care about what happens in the continent, including democratization, particularly when it entails some cost. The North says it cares about the democratization of Africa—but it would appear, not nearly enough. Clearly it is more interested in economic policy reform than democracy, and it is promoting structural adjustment in ways that tend to reinforce political authoritarianism. At the same time, the North continues to collude, often profitably, in making arms available to African governments, arms that are used for repression and that perpetuate underdevelopment. Insofar as the North is interested in democracy, it promotes a kind of democracy whose relevance to Africa is problematic at best and at worst prone to engender contradictions that tend to derail or trivialize democratization in Africa.

The Kind of Democracy Africa Needs

I have discussed the kind of democracy that is unsuitable for Africa rather than the kind that Africa needs. It is time to redress the balance. Taking account of the stated assumptions of the paradigm as well as the social and economic realities of Africa, such as Africa's social pluralism, its poverty, its relatively low level of literacy, and the emphasis in rural communities on solidarity and cooperation, the suitable democracy for Africa would have the following four characteristics:

—A democracy in which people have some real decisionmaking power over and above the formal consent of electoral choice. This will entail, among other things, a powerful legislature, decentralization of power to local democratic formations, and considerable emphasis on the development of institutions for the aggregation and articulation of interests.

—A social democracy that places emphasis on concrete political, social, and economic rights, as opposed to a liberal democracy that emphasizes abstract political rights. It will be a social democracy that invests heavily in the improvement of people's health, education, and capacity so that they can participate effectively.

—A democracy that puts as much emphasis on collective rights as it does on individual rights. It will have to recognize nationalities, subnationalities, ethnic groups, and communities as social formations that express freedom and self-realization and will have to grant them rights to cultural expression and political and economic participation . This could mean, for instance, a second legislative chamber, a "chamber of nationalities," with considerable power in which all nationalities irrespective of their numerical strength are equal. It could mean consociational arrangements, not only at the national level but even at regional and community levels. It will also entail such arrangements as proportional representation and an electoral-spread formula like the one used in Nigeria, by which a party must secure a stipulated minimum percentage of votes over a large part of the country to win.

—A democracy of incorporation. To be as inclusive as possible, the legislative bodies should in addition to nationality groups have special representation of mass organizations, especially youth, the labor movement, and women's groups, which are usually marginalized but without whose active participation there is unlikely to be democracy or development.

Realizing this kind of democracy will depend partly on how far the democratization process is driven by Africans themselves, especially nonelites. What are the prospects of democratization from within? On balance, the prospects are favorable. One reason is the failure of the development project in Africa, which has brought most African governments and ruling elites into disrepute and caused a monumental legitimacy crisis in most of the continent.

The standing of the political elites suffers not only from evident management failure but also from their appearance of neither knowing what to do about the mounting crisis nor being in control of events. They appear exhausted, defeated, and bewildered, and they have ceded the initiative to the international development community, which has also been beaten by the so-called African problem, although still managing to keep the appearance of self-assurance through ideological dogmatism.

The African political elites have been further weakened by the sheer visibility of their lack of control, their poverty of ideas, and their humiliation. Everyone can see the tragic consequences of a grossly mismanaged economy, and everyone can see that those responsible for it do not know how to make amends. Everyone can see how agents of international financial institutions take over significant functions of government, approving tariff regimes, decreeing the level of social services, and deciding on subsidies, privatization, issues of trade, wage levels, the locations of industry, the choice of consultants for government projects, and so forth.

In some countries poorly paid policemen are out of control and openly extort money from citizens. Poorly paid soldiers have become bandits, sealing off isolated country roads and mounting illegal checkpoints to extort money. As if it is not enough to cede control of the economy to foreigners and to lose control over the armed forces, Africa's ruling elites are also losing control of their cities and countryside because of collapsing infrastructure, unserviceable roads, and the encroachment of the forest. The evident helplessness and humiliation of African leaders has emboldened people to defiance.

The structural adjustment programs that African countries have been obliged to adopt are compounding the weakness of the state in Africa owing to their one-sided emphasis on privatization, denationalization, and reliance on market forces. These problems are weakening the state even politically. They are so drastic and so severe in their impact that they engender hostility to the state and undermine its limited legitimacy. In some cases, such as Zambia, Gabon, and Nigeria, they have led to popular insurrections against the state.

Finally, the rigors of the African crisis, especially structural adjustment programs, have forced the masses in Africa to turn away from states that seem helpless in the face of a persistent and deepening crisis, states whose ability to maintain social services and infrastructure are visibly declining or nonexistent. For the most part, people are turning to community organizations, special interest groups, and self-help projects to survive and to arrest the erosion of social services as well as the collapse of the social infrastructure. Even as the state often remains powerful and meddlesome, it is increasingly perceived by its citizens as irrelevant at best, and a nuisance at worst.

The African state is even less likely to be the focus of its citizens' primary loyalty now than it was twenty years ago. To be sure, the weakness of the state and even its displacement does not necessarily translate into a buoyant civil society, a thriving associational life, or democratization, but it improves the prospects of opening alternative political spaces and for waging democratic struggles.

A major asset to democratization in Africa is the growing realization that there is no alternative to participative development. At the Bretton Woods Committee meeting in Washington in April 1990 the president of the World Bank, Barber Conable, listed better governance as the primary requirement for economic recovery in Africa. The World Bank's African blueprint, *Sub-Saharan Africa: From Crisis to Sustainable Growth* (1989), highlights the necessity of accountability, participation, and consensus building for development. And the Bank's press clips on the report show that this view has won approval all over the world.

A conference of more than five hundred groups representing nongovernmental grass-roots organizations, UN agencies, and government, which convened in Arusha, Tanzania, in February 1990 under the auspices of the UN Economic Commission for Africa (UNECA), resulted in the African Charter for Popular Participation in Development and Transformation. The Charter points out that the absence of democracy is the main cause of the chronic crisis in Africa. A speech by the UN secretary-general Javier Pérez de Cuéllar at the Arusha conference argued an inescapable link between economic recovery in Africa and participation. A declaration called *The Political and Socio-Economic Situation in Africa and the Fundamental Changes Taking Place in the World*, which was adopted by the twenty-sixth summit of the Organization of African Unity, held in Addis Ababa, July 9–11, 1990, acknowledged that a political environment that guarantees human rights and the rule of law would be more conducive to accountability and probity than is the present environment and that "popular-based political processes would ensure the involvement of all . . . in development efforts."

Africa's Struggle for Democracy

The foregoing are as yet only theoretical explorations of the feasibility of democratization in Africa. But what are the realities on the ground? What is the actual state of the struggle for democracy in Africa?

A strong movement for democracy is firmly in place in Africa, and it has had considerable success. Just a decade ago, military rule, one-party systems, and personal rule were the standard fare in Africa. Now they are the exception rather than the rule. An impressive number of African countries can boast of electoral competition, constitutionalism, popular participation, and a respectable human rights record: Botswana, Cape Verde, Senegal, Namibia, Mali, Zambia, Gambia, Mauritius, Benin, and São Tomé and Principe. Many more have made attempts at democratic transition. These include Nigeria, Ghana, Cameroon, Angola, Tanzania, Niger, Congo, Burkina Faso, Mauritania, Guinea-Bissau, Ivory Coast, Togo, Mozambique, Kenya, Lesotho, and Seychelles. Most of these have turned out to be false starts; the democratization has often been shallow. But a few, especially Benin and South Africa, have been remarkably successful. Several countries, such as Zaire, are still holding out. But the pressures for democratization are so strong that for most of Africa it is no longer a question of whether there will be a democratic transition but when.

By 1989 authoritarian regimes were being challenged all over Africa, and popular demonstrations for political liberalization and democracy were commonplace. By 1990 there was no doubt that a fundamental political change was taking place as the popular pressures for political reform grew in intensity and spread. In 1989 thirty-eight of the forty-five countries of Sub-Saharan Africa were being ruled either by an autocrat, the military, or a single party. By 1994 military or de facto military regimes had become a curiosity; all but a handful of African countries are now at some stage of democratic transition.

In 1990, a watershed in the democracy movement in Africa, there were popular uprisings in fourteen countries for liberalization and democracy. In Ivory Coast, demonstrations in February and May 1990 demanded a multiparty system. In Zaire, an innocuous forum for political dialogue that President Mobutu Sese Seko had allowed as a way of diffusing political frustration criticized Mobutu and his government vehemently. By May there were violent demonstrations for a multiparty system.

In Zambia, riots broke out as people demanded an end to one-party rule, prompting the government to promise a referendum on the issue. In August 1990 Mozambique's government was obliged to promise multi-

ns in 1991; Angola had already accepted the principle of a
party system in June 1990. In Kenya, riots broke out in July
test against political monolithism and President Moi's disregard
of law. In Cameroon, political tension rose in February 1990
following a lawyers' strike in February to protest the arrest and trial of
Albert Mukong, a dissident. When Yondo Black, the former head of the
Cameroon bar, was arrested for allegedly forming an opposition party in
February 1990, people began to call openly for a multiparty election.
Kenya endured days of rioting in July 1990, after the arrest of two prominent advocates of pluralism, Kenneth Matiba and Charles Rubia.

It would appear that the majority of African leaders initially reacted to
the democratization demands by making the minimal reforms that would,
they hoped, deradicalize the movement. More often than not this took
the form of administrative reforms in the exercise of the autocrat's personal power or political reform of the ruling party: for instance, Moi's
Commission on the Reform of KANU (Kenyan African National Union);
President Gnassingbe Eyadema's restructuring of the ruling party in Togo
in January 1990; President Kenneth Kaunda's dismissal of his cabinet and
the reshuffling of provincial governors in June 1990; Jerry Rawlings's
institution of decentralization; the resignation of President Mobutu as head
of the Popular Movement of the Revolution (MPR), and the revocation of
the ban on opposition parties in April 1990; and the abandonment of the
doctrine of the supremacy of the party in Benin in December 1989 and
in the Congo in July 1990. But these failed to contain the surge of the
democratic revolution. Even leaders like Rawlings, Eyadema, Biya, and
Moi who took the hard line found the pressures unrelenting and eventually
accepted multiparty elections. In each of these cases, the movement
became more insistent. All of them have been forced to concede, to
accept the multiparty system. Some like Biya and Eyadema have tried
to maintain power through a spurious democratic legitimacy of rigged
elections, but that has not removed the pressure for democracy.

Most leaders in Africa have already found the pressures too strong for
token gestures and have had to go along with substantial reform. In Benin,
Mattieu Kerekou, who had hoped to contain the democracy movement,
lost control after the initiation of the National Conference of Active Forces
and eventually lost his presidency in a popular election. In Ivory Coast,
Felix Houphouët-Boigny, who had hoped to deal with the demand for
pluralism with cosmetic changes, was eventually obliged to introduce a
multiparty system, fight an election, and suffer considerable loss of prestige. Mobutu has had to release political prisoners and to accept a multi-

party system and electoral competition, although he still expects to manipulate the multiparty system and the election to ensure his survival in power. President Kaunda, who so adamantly opposed pluralism, eventually reconciled himself to a multiparty system and electoral competition. He fought an election and was resoundingly voted out of power. Zimbabwe has at last ended the state of emergency in effect since independence and has released all political prisoners. President Robert Mugabe found to his disappointment that even his own party, ZANU-PF (Zimbabwe African National Union-Patriotic Front), did not support his bid to change Zimbabwe into a one-party state, and in September 1990 he set aside his plans to make it a one-party state. In March 1990 Madagascar legalized a multiparty system; Niger did the same in July 1990. One of Africa's longest-serving autocrats, President Moussa Traore of Mali, was forced out of office in March 1991 after twenty-three years in office.

Some of the gains of democratization have been remarkable, particularly the peaceful transition to nonracial democracy in South Africa. Also notable is the successful transition to multiparty democracy in Malawi. Against all odds Mozambique had a successful multiparty election in 1994, and the prospects for further institutionalization of democracy look good.

There have been remarkable reversals too, notably in Nigeria, Togo, Gambia, Rwanda, Zaire, Sudan, and Angola. With few exceptions the democratization has been shallow; typically, it takes the form of multiparty elections that are really more of a democratic process than a democratic outcome. Authoritarian state structures remain, accountability to the governed is weak, and the rule of law is sometimes nominal. More often than not, people are voting without choosing.

Most of Africa is still far from liberal democracy and further still from the participative social democracy that our paradigm envisages. However, there has been some impetus toward this particular kind of democracy.

The impetus lies mainly in the internal motivation for democratization in Africa. The surge for democratization arises largely from the failure of development strategies in Africa and the politics associated with them. As noted earlier, in most of Africa, development was launched as an ideological blind by a leadership that was alienated and discredited. In their alienation African leaders became so repressive that the people began to see the state and its development agents as enemies to be evaded, cheated, or defeated, as circumstances permitted. In this atmosphere African leaders were obliged to operate with a siege mentality. They became so absorbed in mere survival that everything else, including development, was marginalized.

These circumstances were more conducive to regression than development, and that is precisely what occurred. The average annual growth rate of per capita income for Sub-Saharan Africa between 1973 and 1980 was a minimal 0.1 percent; between 1980 and 1989 it was -2.2 percent. On some social indicators Africans are worse off today than they were twenty years ago. While the development project floundered, political repression flourished.

That is the background of the democracy movement in Africa. It opposes authoritarian elitism and the construction of development as a strategy of power and exploitation. It is bent on eliminating a leadership whose apparent incompetence and exploitative practices have become life threatening, a threat amply illustrated in Zaire, where per capita income in real terms is only a fraction of what it was when President Mobutu came to power twenty-seven years ago. Finally, the democracy movement in Africa is trying to initiate the kind of politics that will make development possible.

The movement does not yet have an articulated political theory. From what can be pieced together, the movement views the economic regression of Africa as the other side of political repression. It insists that the cause of development is better served by a more democratic approach that engages the energy and the commitment of the people, who alone can make development sustainable. Its theory posits the inescapable connection of the political and the economic, and the priority of the political. That came out clearly in the Arusha conference. The African Charter for Popular Participation argues that the absence of democracy is the main cause of the crisis of underdevelopment in Africa:

We affirm that nations cannot be built without the popular support and full participation of the people, nor can the economic crisis be resolved and the human and economic conditions improved without the full and effective contribution, creativity and popular enthusiasm of the vast majority of the people. After all, it is to the people that the very benefits of development should and must accrue. We are convinced that neither can Africa's perpetual economic crisis be overcome, nor can a bright future for Africa and its people see the light of day unless the structure, pattern and political context of the process of socio-economic development are appropriately altered.

We therefore have no doubt that at the heart of Africa's development objectives must lie the ultimate and overriding good of human-centered development that ensures the overall well-being of the people through sustained improvement in their living standards and the full and effective participation of the people in charting their development policies, programmes and processes and contributing to their realization. We furthermore observe that given the current world political and economic situation, Africa is becoming further marginalized in world affairs, both geo-politically and economically. African countries must realize that, more than ever before, their greatest resource is their people and that it is through their active and full participation that Africa can surmount the difficulties that lie ahead.[4]

In that passage one finds the awareness that gives urgency to the democracy movement in Africa: the notion that Africa's economic problems are rooted in its politics and that a democratic revolution is needed to beat the crisis of underdevelopment. Africans are seeking democracy as a matter of survival; they believe that there are no alternatives to this quest, that they have nothing to lose and a great deal to gain. This awareness has grown in recent years as it has become more and more obvious that neither the indigenous political elites nor the multilateral development agencies are capable of dealing with the African crisis.

Insofar as the democracy movement in Africa gets its impetus from the social and economic aspirations of people in Africa yearning for "a second independence from their leaders," it will be markedly different from liberal democracy. In all probability it will emphasize concrete economic and social rights rather than abstract political rights; it will insist on the democratization of economic opportunities, the social betterment of the people, and a strong social welfare system. To achieve these goals, it will have to be effectively participative and will have to draw on African traditions to adapt democracy to the cultural and historical experience of ordinary people.

Such a people-driven democratization, however, will continue to be challenged by the elite-driven democratization that reduces democracy to multiparty electoral competition and generally exploits it as a strategy of power. It is by no means clear that the people-driven democracy will prevail. But it has a fair chance.

The Development Strategy

Development strategy is not a matter of drawing up an ideal blueprint but rather one of pragmatically devising a way of proceeding within the

4. UNECA (1990, pp. 17–18).

constraints and possibilities of the realities on the ground, the realities that have been articulated and analyzed in the preceding chapters. The realities themselves are multifaceted, complicated, elusive, and in some respects contradictory, all of which suggests that proceeding by paying attention to the realities on the ground is not saying much. But they have been structured in the course of my analysis, insofar as the analysis has suggested which tendencies in the pursuit of development are desirable and which are undesirable and established a few principles or guidelines that need to be put into operation and some values that should be maximized. Before continuing the discussion of development strategy, I summarize these values and principles.

A popular development strategy. The primary principle of development strategy in Africa is that the people have to be the agents, the means, and the end of development. This principle is the underpinning of all development policies; their mechanisms of implementation and the distribution of the benefits of development are fairly obvious.

Self-reliance. To own their own development, people have to be self-reliant. As I have tried to show in the preceding pages, development cannot be received; it has to be experienced as participation in the process of bringing it about. In the past, self-reliance has been largely a posture against foreign domination, a protest against being dependent and in the control of foreigners. This concept is pertinent, but it misses the crucial point of self-reliance.

Self-reliance is about responsibility: in the context of development, responsibility for producing a development project as well as providing the resources to carry it through. The embracing of self-reliance will be the real revolution of development in Africa. It is true that Africa's colonial history and its place in the world system have not been conducive to independence. But the other side of the coin is that, with minor exceptions, African leaders have preferred a cozy accommodation with dependence than the rigors of self-reliance, and they have usually accentuated dependence by their policies and behavior instead of reducing it. Breaking away from this colonial mentality and the lack of independence associated with it is as difficult as it is necessary.

To realize development, self-reliance has to be practiced at all levels. Starting from the level of national policies and the relation between states, it must also spread to the level of regions, federal units (where they exist), communities, and households. At these local levels, too, the habit of dependence is very strong and somewhat contradicts the demand for local autonomy. And poverty and the weak sense of efficacy often associated with it tend to compound the problem. But whatever the difficulties of self-reliance, it is nonetheless true that only when it is taken seriously at every level can development become feasible.

Empowerment and confidence. Self-reliance requires much confidence. Lack of confidence is a serious problem; it may well be the greatest obstacle to the development of Africa. The problem is very deep and goes back a long way. To justify their barbaric assault on Africa, those who colonized it had to insist that Africans were less than human. They then proceeded to reduce Africans to a condition in which they would deserve to be colonized, deserve the dubious redemption of the civilizing mission. The humiliations of colonization in the colonial era, and the slavery before it, virtually destroyed the confidence of Africans, especially educated urban Africans.

Matters have not been helped by the performance of most African leaders in three decades of independence. With few exceptions their rule has been notable for oppression, corruption, social disorganization, the demise of the development project, and growing poverty. The performance reinforces the negative view of Africa in a vicious circle of negativity and diminishing self-esteem. By all indications, despite the brave talk about forging ahead through a sea of problems, most African leaders are demoralized. But development is a historical enterprise that requires high seriousness and enormous self-confidence, qualities extremely difficult to attain in Africa's present circumstances.

This confidence will not be created by posturing against former colonial masters or by verbal exhortations. It will require something more tangible, especially increasing capabilities and concrete achievement. It will have to be created on substantive success, in particular the success of self-reliant development projects at every level of the society. It is helpful if, initially, success is perceivable in the material improvement of the lot of people involved in the development project. The development strategy for Africa will also have to be a strategy for incremental improvement of capabilities and self-esteem at all levels of society.

Self-realization rather than alienation. If the people possess their own development, the development process will not turn into an exercise in alienation, as has been the case in much of Africa. What is happening now is an attempt to develop *against* the people—a strategy characterized by appropriating the people's right to develop themselves.

As noted, the old strategies assume all too readily that the people and their way of life is the problem, so that attacking the problem blends into attacking the people and their way of life. When the people themselves are made the problem, rather than the process of development, development is derailed. At that point it becomes an exercise in alienation at best and a violent assault on people at worst.

What is needed is to move away from the fixation on how Africa ought to be and how to force-feed Africa into that state of being. Development must take the people not as they ought to be but as they are and try to find how the people can move forward by their own efforts, in accordance with their own values.

Agricultural Strategy

If the people are the agents, the means and the end of development, then development has to be construed initially as rural development generally and more specifically as agricultural development. More than 70 percent of the peoples of Africa are rural dwellers who get their livelihood largely from agricultural activity. It is in agricultural activity that they can immediately participate in economic development; it is the sphere in which they have skills and experience to offer and in which they can most profit by enhancement. But there are other reasons for conceiving development initially as agricultural development, reasons clearly stated in a 1993 World Bank study:

Other productive sectors are relatively small. Agriculture provided 32 percent of Gross Domestic Product (GDP) on average in 1990. Without agricultural growth at 4 percent per annum, the generally most competitive industrial sector (agro-industry) will not be supplied with the raw material to permit it to grow by its target rate of 5 to 7 percent per annum. Analysis undertaken for Sub-Saharan Africa (SSA) found that agricultural growth is the most important contributor to the growth of manufacturing and services. Agriculture is the major source of raw material for industry, is a main purchaser of simple tools (farm implements), is a purchaser of services (farm mechanics, transport), and farmers are the main consumers of consumption goods produced locally. Agricultural production will remain the most important element for addressing food security and poverty, since most of the poor and the food-insecure are rural people. Agriculture is the largest private sector in Africa. Stimulating the private sector means stimulating agriculture and agriculturally-related industry. Improving the well-being of women, whose principal economic activity remains farming, means in large part helping them to become better farmers.[5]

The study then outlines a strategy of agricultural development. It says that "the pillar of a new strategy is to undertake policy change necessary to make agriculture, agro-industry and related services profitable. This profitability will be the main element to stimulate the private sector (including small farmers) to invest in agriculture, agro-industry, livestock, marketing, input supply, and credit."[6]

What is needed is not a strategy whose overriding concern or thrust is to make agriculture profitable. Rather, what is needed is a strategy that encourages farmers to do what they are doing better, to be more efficient and more productive, a strategy that is conducive to the realization of those interests that led them to farming in the first place. Encouraging farmers to do better also entails empowering them, making them more skillful, more confident, giving them more access to the things they need to be more efficient. This can be done in several ways.

Bringing the farmer to the center. The first element of this strategy is for the farmer to move to the center of agricultural policy. An essential preliminary is to initiate a policy dialogue among farmers, and between farmers and officials, on the need, the desirability, and means of improving the efficiency and productivity of farmers and increasing the benefits that accrue to them from farming. This dialogue could be held at all levels— groups of households, communities, villages, cooperatives, farmers' associations, rural improvement associations, and so forth. It should be open-ended so that the farmers have a real opportunity to make decisions instead of participating only to legitimize the preconceptions of officials. If the dialogue proceeds in this way, the problem of agricultural development begins to be a problem of the farmers rather than that of ministry officials, and when solutions emerge, they will also be the farmers' own solutions. They will be responsible for the success or failure of development; they will understand their risks and benefits and will be highly motivated to increase the latter.

Bringing in the farmers to the center of policy will also remove the constraints that prevent them from taking charge or even participating effectively. These constraints include the regulation of what the farmers can produce, when and how they can produce it, what they can sell, where they may sell and for how much. These constraints have not only

5. Cleaver (1993, p. 7).
6. Cleaver (1993, p. 7).

marginalized farmers; they have proved to be a strong disincentive to agricultural productivity.

Infrastructure support for farming activities. In Africa the ability of farmers to do what they are already doing more efficiently will require improving rural infrastructure, especially roads, water supply, electricity, markets, transportation, and energy. The history of agricultural development in every part of the world, including East Asia and India, underlines the special importance of rural infrastructure. Supporters of infrastructure improvement in rural Africa make the same point. A good example is the surge in agricultural growth in Nigeria in the late 1980s as a result of the creation of the Directorate of Food, Roads and Rural Infrastructure (DFRRI).

Somehow rural infrastructure in Africa has continued to be grossly neglected despite wide knowledge of its impact on agricultural development. For instance, it is estimated that in West Africa rural road density is only about 32 m/km^2, and only 36 m/km^2 in eastern and southern Africa. In contrast, parts of India with comparative population densities have a road density of about 730 m/km^2.[7] Rural infrastructure was poor enough but has greatly deteriorated in the past decade as a result of the fiscal crisis of African states.

One serious problem is that most rural families in Africa do not have easy access to safe water. The water provider of the family, usually a woman, could easily spend as many as two hours a day on the chore of fetching water. Fetching firewood, also usually done by a woman, takes about as much time. Therefore, just obtaining water and basic energy, which should be taken for granted, reduce a woman's farming activities and her productivity.

It is necessary to acknowledge the serious resource constraints on the improvement of rural infrastructure in Africa. These constraints will not allow wholesale improvement in the short to medium term. Nonetheless, considerable improvement can be made by correcting the elite-urban bias in development expenditures. Also, the constraints can serve a positive function by compelling more imaginative thinking; for example, the use of community effort to provide infrastructure that expresses the people's self-reliance and possession of their own development. Self-reliant development of rural infrastructure will in turn enhance rural capabilities and confidence and improve the prospects of adequate maintenance of that infrastructure.

7. Cleaver (1993, p. 83).

Technology. To do what they are already doing better, African agricultural producers need better technologies. The scope for improving farmers' productivity is enormous, since their level of technological backing is currently very low, often inappropriate, and made available in ways that are frequently counterproductive.

Here again the critical factor is putting the farmer in charge. Everybody, including the World Bank and the IMF, recognizes the need to elicit the participation of farmers. This concern is evident in several World Bank publications.[8] But this awareness has not had the policy impact that it might be expected to have.

The concept of participation needs to be translated into that of "centering" the farmer. Current participative approaches are still limited to consulting, eliciting input, helping, and empowering. All these are desirable, but they need to go further, to centering. In the context of the issue under consideration here, namely, enhancing agricultural productivity by technology, the first point is for farmers to own their development, including the means by which it is pursued. As noted, the process of owning development is an important aspect of what it means to be developing.

In the sphere of technology policy for agricultural development, it is easy to reduce the notion of "centering" the farmer to the formality of perfunctory consultation with or responsiveness to farmers, partly because of presumptions about technology's being a sphere of expertise and about the ignorance of farmers in this area. Because of these dispositions it is necessary to clarify what putting the farmers in charge entails. Doing so does not romanticize farmers; it does not assume that their knowledge and practices are always right. It assumes not only that their views will be decisive but also that any particular view will be tested and amended as desirable, if possible by interaction with the views of other farmers and specialists such as agronomists and extension workers.

Taking farmers seriously must also mean assuming that, like everyone else, they are sometimes misguided, mistaken, confused, and self-defeating even in pursuing what they perceive to be their interests. The extension worker may well have better knowledge about certain aspects of farming, but it is the farmer who is doing the farming and whose development is at issue; it is up to the specialist to convince the farmer to adopt his or her idea. Ideas so adopted in open-ended equal exchange do not compromise the principle of centering the farmer. But they are not compatible

8. See, for example, *Technology for Small-Scale Farmers in Sub-Saharan Africa* (1989); *Implementing the World Bank's Strategy to Reduce Poverty* (1993); and *A Strategy to Develop Agriculture in Sub-Saharan Africa, and a Focus for the World Bank* (1993).

with extension service bureaucracies. Extension services need to be integrated into farmers' organizations as special units accountable to the organizations.

The other side of possessing development is being responsible for its costs. This principle is incompatible with dependence on government handouts. Even in rural agriculture and among poor farmers who are barely surviving, the principle of self-reliance should be built into strategies for making the farmer more productive. Possessing development entails paying for it. Even poor farmers should "pay"; they should be self-reliant as much as possible even if it means paying in kind, labor, or services. They will take what they are paying for far more seriously; they will be motivated to greater productivity as they try to maximize returns on their investment. Paying enhances self-esteem and empowerment; it means possessing development and taking responsibility. Indeed, paying is an important aspect of what development is. Therefore, it cannot on principle be set aside even among the very poor.

Human resources development. Helping farmers to do better involves more than anything else the continuous enhancement of their quality as a resource for development. That calls for a development strategy which invests in human resource development, especially in education, health, management capabilities, and skill development and improvement. Healthy, educated, and skillful farmers are more productive and are more likely to make income gains and to expand the range of options available to them.

General national investment in social infrastructure, particularly basic services such as primary schools and primary health care, is an asset to agricultural development because the poor, who get a disproportionate share of those benefits, are largely subsistence farmers.

Apart from such national catchall policies, it is also necessary to address the human development needs of groups with special needs, rather on the lines of the World Bank's Program of Targeted Interventions.[9] For instance, most of Africa's farmers are women, but apart from being the farmer, the woman also has the enormous responsibilities of bearing children and managing the household with its time-consuming chores. Women need education relevant to their needs and a health system that addresses their reproductive needs and reproductive health. Given women's demanding multiple roles in Africa, a program of human resource development should also be concerned with saving time and making their

9. See Cleaver (1993).

chores less onerous by simple technologies and better access to services and facilities such as water supply and cheap energy.

Even in the area of social infrastructure, it is necessary to be sensitive to principles of possession and self-reliance. The expectation is not that farmers will on their own design and set up primary health care systems or educational systems and also finance them. If they could do so, it would of course be desirable. What can reasonably be expected is that the human resource units will be accountable to the people who will set their agendas. But the farming organizations and communities also have to be responsible for the successful operation of the human resource units and contribute to it even as they receive from it, as particular historical circumstance permit; for instance, for certain training programs a participant could pay by training another person.

As much as possible, even in conditions of poverty, nothing should be free. To repeat, this principle derives not from attachment to market forces but from the idea that development is, among other things, paying one's way. There is also the practical consideration that paying sets a rigorous standard for social infrastructure projects that will probably eliminate weak projects likely to fail. The benefits of a project have to be clear, concrete, and relevant before ordinary people can bring themselves to pay for it. Needless to say, there are circumstances in which payment will not be feasible, and demand for payment inappropriate.

Selection of Projects by Impact

The breakthrough in development comes when ordinary people become confident that self-development is feasible. A well-conceived development strategy will strive to achieve this threshold as soon as possible. It is all the more important for the people to see the feasibility and fruits of self-development quickly, because they are paying for it. To achieve this threshold quickly, development strategy has to place special emphasis on projects that can have a clear, concrete, and positive impact in the short run; for instance, a macroeconomic framework that removes price distortions that penalize farmers, and supportive extension services, including supply of inputs and food security programs.

However, strategy cannot simply be geared to the short run. The importance of quick results has to be balanced against projects that are critical for agricultural development but that produce benefits more slowly, in the medium term or even the long term. Medium-term projects of, say, one to five years, such as roads, irrigation, land tenure reform, and soil conservation, are too important to be shelved just because their benefits will take longer to realize. Much the same thing might be said for long-term projects like educational and health projects. The need for an immediate impact must be reconciled with the need for longer-term projects. The mix of projects will vary from place to place, reflecting the needs, problems, and prospects of particular situations.

The process of enabling the farmer to do better will also have to be given specificity in terms of the characteristics of the ecological zones that define, often definitively, the constraints on agricultural development and what might be done about it. According to a 1989 World Bank study, there are five broad ecological zones: the humid tropical zone of West and central Africa, where the main constraint on agriculture is soil fertility; the subhumid zone of West Africa, which is sparsely populated and where the major problem is labor supply; the sorghum and millet belt of West Africa, where lack of water is the principal constraint; the savannah zone of eastern and southern Africa, where there are labor-supply problems in the wetter regions and low-rainfall problems in other areas; and the Highlands of eastern Africa, which are very densely populated and suffer from a shortage of land. In the Highlands agricultural development greatly depends on finding and applying technologies that increase the intensity of land use.[10]

The Smallholder Focus

Development strategy cannot be effective unless its implications are worked through institutional settings, including production units, labor institutions, organizational structures, and social and cultural settings. Since most farmers in Africa are smallholder farmers, policy has to begin by focusing on this productive unit and the basic productive unit associated with it—namely, the household economy. The thrust of policy in Africa has been rather hostile to the household economy and smallholder farming, which are considered regressive forms whose disappearance is a necessary condition of economic growth. The household economy, in particular, has been attacked implicitly but determinedly for producing essentially use values rather than exchange values, for hindering the capitalization of agriculture, and for perpetuating a scale of operation and a technological level that are not conducive to high productivity. Whatever its limitations, as long as the household is the basic economic unit in rural

10. Carr (1989, p. xii).

Africa and invariably the institutional basis of smallholder agriculture, development strategy has to accept its validity and build on it.

Building on it will not be without problems. For instance, the extent to which productivity can be increased in the household economy is limited by the cellular structure of households, their independence from one another, their inward orientation, and their limited specialization. Building on that economy will entail dealing with its constraints and changing it. Such change will occur according to the democratic will of those whose life-style is at issue; it will mean not their alienation but their self-development. It will be change without trauma, without external coercion, and in accordance with the desires and interests of the people for whom the household economy is an important way of life.

In the African context, the household economy, though it has not found favor among development managers, is an important indigenous institution that deserves special attention. The features of this economy are interesting. It is an economy concerned with reproduction rather than production, and it follows the law of subsistence rather than the law of value. Because the household economy is such an important part of what Africans are today, development strategies should have been building on it. Indeed, it offers good prospects for sustainable development. Failure to explore it along those lines is rather surprising. The household economy has the characteristics and values that development is supposed to realize for the African economy on the national level, especially self-reliance, internal balance, self-sufficiency, and autocentric dynamics.

The model of the household economy might have helped to avoid one of the appalling disasters of the development experience in Africa; namely, the food dependence of an overwhelmingly rural population that has land of acceptable fertility and adequate grazing. Between 1971 and 1980 agricultural output grew 1.6 percent a year, while population grew 2.8 percent a year; the food self-sufficiency ratio dropped from 98 percent in the 1960s to 86 percent in the 1980s and continued to decline through 1984. Today, 20 percent of Africa's population depends on food imports, which increased at an average annual rate of 8.4 percent between 1970 and 1980.

The African household economy forces attention on food self-sufficiency. That is its natural tendency, since it is concerned with reproduction rather than production and follows the law of subsistence. Given the constraints of the household economy, using the model of this economy on the national level would not have brought an impressive rate of growth. But it would have helped Africa to feed itself. It would have given African economies some internal balance. If a national economy had been moved in these directions, its growth and development, modest as they might be, would at least have been decidedly sustainable, because they would have been largely internalized.

It is important to emphasize that the internalization of growth dynamics is the hallmark of sustainable development, something that is often ignored in theory and practice. Thus prevailing definitions of sustainable development, especially those used by international development agencies, make no reference to autocentric dynamics. At the level of practice, development strategies in Africa display little or no interest in maximizing internal balance and autocentric dynamics. This attitude could be due to the tragic enormity of the African crisis, which has diverted attention to emergency measures for survival. But if the crisis explains emergency programs such as APPER and UNPAAERD, the commanding role of the International Monetary Fund, and structural adjustment programs, it hardly explains why, for instance, the structural adjustment programs are so rigidly bent on external balance instead of internal balance.

Like the household economy, smallholder agriculture has often been regarded as an obstacle to progress, a prejudice heightened by the experience of many countries such as France, Great Britain, and Germany, where rapid economic growth was usually associated with moving away from smallholder farming. The traditional prejudice against smallholder farming and peasants is so strong that considerable violence has often been used to destroy this way of life, the most notable being the enclosure movement in Britain in the nineteenth century and the liquidation of the kulaks by Stalin.

Some analysts believe that Africa cannot begin rapid economic growth until the small farmer is liquidated or "captured."[11] The vast majority of smallholders would not wish their own violent liquidation on the presumed rationality of alien values, but rather would wish the improvement of their lot, taking themselves as they are, not as some development agent might want them to be.

In any event, the case for a smallholder focus is not simply its inevitability as the choice of an essentially smallholder community but its validity as the way of proceeding with development. For if development must take people as they are and regard them as its end, then the smallholder strategy is the proper way to begin.

It is interesting that the smallholder approach has been more successful

11. See, for example, Hyden (1980).

in Africa than the much-favored commercial agriculture. African governments—for instance, Nigeria—are increasingly acknowledging the disastrous outcomes of their ventures into large-scale commercial farming,
although the rising tide of self-criticism hardly leads to radical breaks from
the old policies. To its credit, the World Bank has gone much further
than most African governments in the adoption of a smallholder farm
development policy. What is more, unlike most African governments, the
Bank did not merely drift into that policy but accepted it as a well-reasoned
conclusion. A 1988 study presents this argument:

> In most African countries where nonfarm employment is still limited
> and the opportunity cost of labor is low, the economies of small farm
> size out-weigh the economies of scale. This is primarily because agricul-
> tural production is a biological process spread out in time and in space
> which gives rise to costly problems in recruiting and supervising a
> large work force. Furthermore, centralized decisionmaking and the
> exercise of initiative and judgment is especially important in farming
> in Africa because of the unpredictable variations in weather and other
> exogenous sources of uncertainty. Because family members have a
> claim on the production of the farm rather than receiving a fixed wage,
> they have strong incentives to work hard and exercise initiative and
> judgment. Finally, it needs to be stressed that a major advantage of
> pursuing a broad-based small farm development strategy is that it gener-
> ates a pattern of growth of farm incomes and of effective demand for
> nonfarm goods and services that stimulates more rapid growth of output
> and employment than would be obtained from a large farm strategy.[12]

In practice, the World Bank is somewhat ambivalent, however. It discourages very small farms and investment on farm holdings of the very
poor that are considered "economically inefficient." Apparently what the
Bank really wants are middle-level farms: "The growth of a class of medium-
sized moderately well-off farms is to be encouraged particularly if they
emerge from the smaller farming community, as opposed to absentee
farmers working in urban areas who purchase medium-sized land holdings
which they proceed to operate inefficiently."[13]

Constraints of the Smallholder Approach

The smallholder approach is by no means an ideal local unit for agricultural development. It has some constraints. To begin with, it can be a

12. Vyas and Casley (1988, pp. 28–29).
13. Vyas and Casley (1988, p. 28).

difficult, complex, and expensive approach in African conditions. For instance, it needs many supporting organizational structures: farmers' organizations at all levels, joint committees of farmers' groups and extension workers, cooperatives, self-help projects, and so on. Apart from that, a large number of institutions will be needed to service those structures, and this may mean a proliferation of agricultural development-related institutions of government, nongovernmental organizations, international development agencies, international financial institutions, and so forth. The complexity and multiplicity of such organizations and the slow pace of democratic arrangements cause some resistance to the strategy of this development policy option. Although these problems may be reduced, they cannot be eliminated, for they are inherent in the strategy of making development a living experience.

The values of the agricultural strategy of the paradigm that have been outlined here assume the necessity and desirability of smallholder agriculture. That comes from the commitment of taking people as they are and not as they ought to be. To do so does not imply that smallholder agriculture will be sustainable in the future or even that it is desirable that it should be. The point is to recognize that some smallholder farming is the material base of the lives of most Africans and to build on it. The assumption is that development ought to be democratic and allow rural people to improve the situation they have instead of abolishing it for an uncertain alternative. Unlike a policy that tried to make agriculture profitable by unleashing market forces, the smallholder approach would be more tolerant of the inefficiencies caused by intervention against the market, as might be necessary from time to time. Those inefficiencies can be a serious problem, considering the meagerness of the resources of African countries. But the problem is mitigated to some degree by the fact that the strategy recommended here puts emphasis on paying, even by the poor—paying in spite of the strain of doing so, since the experience of self-reliance is part of what development is.

Another problem is that the emphasis on the privileges of smallholder farming offers limited scope for the realization of economies of scale. Not only that, the scale of smallholder agriculture might discourage the use of certain useful technologies such as tractors. But this problem is not as serious as it seems. It can be reduced somewhat by aggregating people into bigger units such as cooperatives for the purpose of sharing technologies, extension serves, collecting centers, and physical infrastructure.

Furthermore, the limitation of scale of smallholder farming and the land tenure systems associated with it could in one sense be an important advantage. If improvements create a demand for more farmland that cannot be met, attention is likely to be directed to intensification. A prime cause of the Green Revolution in Asia was the need for intensity arising from a shortage of land. In Africa, land scarcity, with notable exceptions, was not a problem until the 1980s; the shifting of cultivation associated with land abundance has hitherto discouraged agricultural intensity. Now shifting cultivation is being rapidly abandoned, and the move to intensity has already begun, with some promising results in Kenya, Nigeria, and Zimbabwe, for instance. The scale constraints of the smallholder strategy and diminishing land availability are also opportunities for technological intensity, which has enormous potential for developing agriculture in Africa.

Finally, small-scale farming is not advocated to the exclusion of everything else, especially large-scale commercial farming. What is important is that agricultural policy should generate the impetus to development by concentrating resources at the base, that is, on farmers who are overwhelmingly smallholder farmers. There is no objection to large-scale agriculture in principle. The practical objection to it is that, reflecting the elitist bent in African development strategies, large-scale farming and even large-scale agricultural parastatals have tended to attract a grossly disproportionate share of the development budget going to agriculture, and they have usually been too inefficient to justify the resources going into them. If large private farmers could be efficient and profitable without requiring enormous public expenditure to create and maintain their "enabling environment," they would be very useful.

Indeed, such commercial farms could be supportive of the smallholder farming community in important ways; for instance, intervening in national policy to ensure a macroeconomic framework favorable to agricultural development. They would open up national and international markets, develop the labor market, and stimulate the development of agricultural infrastructure, agricultural research, and agricultural technology; they would promote the linking of agricultural development and industrialization by their demand for technologies and their expansion into agro-based industries such as food processing.

Rural Industrialization

If, as suggested here, one assimilates the concept of development into the idea of rural development, the traditional dichotomy between agriculture and industrialization will tend to disappear. Industrialization will then begin as rural industrialization, a part of the process of rural development.

The failure to proceed in this manner has been a serious impediment to agricultural and industrial development in Africa. Prevailing strategies have been concerned with import substitution, export promotion, and huge basic industrial projects like iron and steel and petrochemicals. A policy of rural industrialization integrated with agricultural development as part of a strategy of rural development would be a better alternative. Industrialization would be pursued mainly on the basis of self-reliance, fueled primarily from the incomes of farmers and the multiplier effect of the linkages between farm and nonfarm activities.

Immense opportunities exist for improving agricultural technology to the benefit of both agriculture and industrialization. For centuries African agriculture has been dominated by hoes, wooden paddles for threshing, and machetes. New simple technologies such as seeders, ox-plows, and inter-row weeders could be introduced. Being scale neutral, they could be manufactured in small lots, locally, to the advantage of farmers and rural industrialization.

There are forward linkages as well; for example, food processing, brewing, and packaging. The untapped potential here is enormous. Finally, there are large opportunities in consumer-demand linkages. Rises in farm incomes increase the demand for consumer goods such as shoes, clothes, furniture, building materials, and new kinds of food. This demand promotes industrialization, and the availability of the consumer goods provides a strong incentive for increased agricultural productivity.

As these forward, backward, and consumer-demand linkages expand, there will be greater integration of rural and urban development. Urban development will at first be primarily about the informal sector, which employs the vast majority of urban dwellers in Africa. As with rural industrialization, the concern is to enable people to be more productive in what they are doing, to encourage movement to higher technological levels. The levels of education and technology are the same. Rural industries and the informal sector will be producing similar goods under roughly similar conditions for the same market.

This approach to industrialization will markedly improve the possibility of development. It proceeds in daily response to the practical needs of the people; it is endogenous and self-reliant; it is not driven by foreign loans, foreign technology, foreign investment, or foreign trade; it relies on an assured and gradually expanding domestic market; it obliterates the dichotomy between industry and agriculture, urban and rural, and promotes internal balance and autocentrism.

Complementary Policies

Clearly, by conventional standards, "inefficiencies" exist in this strategy: for instance, its call for participation could be time consuming and expensive. It could engender a multiplicity of institutions with complicated relations. At the level considered here, education is low, physical infrastructure is very poor or nonexistent, savings are low or nonexistent, and effective demand is low. Such are hardly the conditions that will lead to rapid economic growth in the short or medium term.

However, these factors may be "inefficiencies" relative to the goal of economic growth but not relative to development. They are part of what it takes to put development into operation, a lived experience in which the people are the agents, the means, and the ends of social transformation for their greater well-being. Nonetheless, it is desirable that a clear commitment to development in that sense is, as much as possible, reconciled to more rapid economic growth.

The sector of smallholder farms is usually marginal in African economies. Control of African economies tends to be vested in the urban enclaves, especially in the hands of government, a small private sector, and multinationals. The strategy advocated here presupposes democratization of sufficient depth to overcome not only the urban bias in African development strategies but also a drastic shift in development expenditures away from the urban enclaves to the rural areas. That will be difficult. The indications are that, although the rural share of development expenditures will increase, the bulk of the economic surplus will be in the control of the leaders of the urban enclaves.

While the relationship between these enclaves might have been exploitative in the past, it need not be so. If the politics and economic policies are right, these enclaves will complement the rural sector and contribute to the acceleration of its economic growth. The management of the more powerful enclave economy has to be an important part of the strategy of the residual option. These will include:

—Creating a stable macroeconomic framework that will provide positive incentives to farmers.

—Attracting strategic foreign direct investment, which will give countries more access to capital, managerial know-how, and technology. This is all the more necessary because large commercial borrowing is not a viable option for African countries in view of their indebtedness, debt crisis, and unstable macroeconomic framework.

—Engineering competitiveness through better infrastructure and appropriate exchange rate, tariff regime, and labor market policies.

—Providing carefully targeted government intervention to assist export industries.

—Encouraging policies that reconcile growth with distribution, as was the case in East Asia.

Such policies greatly contributed to the phenomenal growth of the East Asian countries, as the World Bank's *The East Asian Miracle* (1993) has shown. But Africa's conditions, especially political constraints on the adoption of these policies, underscore once more the political underpinnings of the persistence of underdevelopment in Africa. One remarkable feature of development in East Asia was a de facto social compact made among the elites and between the elites and the people: "First, leaders had to convince economic elites to support pro-growth policies. Then they had to persuade the elites to share the benefits of growth with the middle class and the poor. Finally, to win the cooperation of the middle class and the poor, the leaders had to show them that they would indeed benefit from future growth."[14]

The political class had a clear development project and the discipline to carry out this elaborate social compact, achieving the best record ever of growth with distribution: "For the eight HPAEs [high-performing Asian economies], rapid growth and declining inequality have been shared virtues, as comparisons over time of equality and growth . . . illustrate. The developing HPAEs clearly outperform other middle income economies in that they have both lower levels of inequality and higher levels of growth. Moreover improvements in income distribution generally coincided with periods of rapid growth."[15]

The distributive growth was achieved by a mix of policies with varying emphasis in each country. All of them invested heavily in human capital, especially in education and health. For instance, in South Korea, expenditure per pupil in real terms rose by 355 per cent between 1970 and 1989. Investment is redistributive because the poor benefit disproportionally more from investment in basic social infrastructure, including benefits in upward mobility. Distribution was also pursued through land reform. In China and Taiwan land was taken from landlords with some compensation

14. World Bank (1993b, p. 13).
15. World Bank (1993b, p. 30).

and sold to the tillers on favorable terms such as easy credit. In South Korea, in 1947 the government redistributed land originally held by the Japanese rulers of the country, and beginning in 1950 the government took over land from landlords and distributed it to 900,000 tenants. Redistribution also took the form of generous support for small-scale and medium-scale enterprises, support that was both distributive and productive. Some of the HPAEs redistributed through social welfare programs such as public housing, in particular Singapore and Hong Kong. By 1987 "more than 40 percent of the population in Hong Kong lived in public housing"; in Singapore, "today, 80 percent of the population lives in public housing and more than 90 percent of the families in public housing own their units."[16]

Distributive growth was only one aspect of the discipline of the political class in East Asia in pursuing the development project. Discipline was also evident in the creation of a class of highly competent technocrats to manage the project, insulating them politically, according them high social status, and giving them room to be creative in a strict meritocracy. It was evident even in the interventions of the political class in the economy; for instance, special incentives to business, especially in the export sector, were granted on a competitive basis and maintained on the basis of performance.

These kinds of policies would not be possible under most governments in contemporary Africa, even with the best of intentions. The political class in Africa typically lacks coherence. More often than not, it is riddled with factionalism and strong centrifugal tendencies associated with the inculcation of parochial loyalties that are exploited for economic and political power. The public sphere is a battlefield where parochial groups and interest groups struggle for power relentlessly, and sometimes violently. In this context, the state is chronically unstable, usually privatized, corrupt, and inefficient, and largely incapable of carrying out a development project.

So a huge political gap exists between the African and the East Asian experience. This difference says something about the importance of political variables, since, even within authoritarian political systems, political differences can make critical differences in the prospects for economic growth.

In East Asia, political authoritarianism has been associated with a crystallized political class that is highly disciplined and is in turn able to maintain

16. World Bank (1993b, pp. 163–64).

discipline in polity and economy. More important, this political class was highly committed to the development project and so disciplined that it was able to realize some of the economically functional values of democracy such as accountability, transparency, the rule of law, and negotiated consensus. For instance, the social compact that promoted growth with equity in this region was a product of negotiated consensus as well as a sense of accountability to the public interest. In all eight countries, economic incentives, such as special export credits, have been granted on markedly transparent and competitive procedures. The way in which all the countries have maintained financial discipline and a stable competition-oriented macroeconomic framework attests to a basic commitment to the rule of law and the relative autonomy of the state.

In Africa, political authoritarianism has been detrimental to economic growth and even political stability. It has been associated with arbitrariness, lack of transparency, rent seeking, and the dissociation of performance from reward.

Appearances notwithstanding, however, the response to this situation should be not a more development-friendly authoritarianism in Africa but democratization. For if the rule of law, transparency, accountability, equity, and consensus building are desirable, they should not be contingent on the will of the elites, as was true in much of East Asia. It is better to have arrangements that render their realization objectively necessary. And that is what democracy does, albeit with limitations. Besides, democracy is part of what development is about, and as noted, it cannot wait.

Conclusion

Sub-Saharan Africa is mired in one of the deepest and most protracted crises of modern history. This crisis has been phenomenally harsh, tragic, and demoralizing. But it has also been an invaluable learning experience. It has taught Africa a great deal about how not to go about development and even a little about how to do it. Pushed to the brink, ordinary people in Africa have apparently realized that they must take their destiny into their own hands, and they are struggling for a "second independence." They have apparently recognized that they cannot escape from underdevelopment until public policy becomes an expression of their democratic will and connects again with social needs.

Not many people view the development of Africa as a viable proposition. This is not surprising. The world has been mesmerized by the dismal statistics of declining productivity and growth rates, escalating indebtedness, and chronic malnutrition, famine, and disease. The high incidence of political instability and violent conflict in some parts of Africa, such as Burundi, Rwanda, Liberia, Somalia, Sudan, and Sierra Leone, has not helped matters. Nevertheless, the development project has not failed in Africa. It just never started in the first place because of hostile political conditions. It can start and it can succeed. The disasters of the past have been useful lessons, awareness is developing, and objective conditions in the world now make self-reliance increasingly inevitable and desirable; ordinary people are in revolt and demanding a second independence. They are struggling to take control of their own lives from a leadership whose mismanagement has become life threatening for them. The struggle over the political framework that will enable the development project to finally take off is now in progress, and the prospects for development are promising.

References

Adedeji, Adebajo. 1988. "A Preliminary Assessment of the Performance of the African Economy in 1987 and Prospects for 1988." Address to Corps Diplomatique and the International Community. Addis Ababa, Ethiopia, January 4.

———. 1990. "Dimensions of the African Crisis." Keynote Address to the Conference on the Economic Crisis in Africa, October 25–28.

Ake, Claude. 1985. "Indigenization: Problems of Transformation in a Neocolonial Economy." In *Political Economy of Nigeria*, edited by Claude Ake, 173–200. London: Longman.

———. 1991. "Rethinking African Democracy." *Journal of Democracy* 2 (Winter): 32–44.

Almond, Gabriel A., and Sidney Verba. 1963, 1980. *The Civil Culture: Political Attitudes and Democracy in Five Nations*. Princeton University Press.

Apter, David E. 1965. *The Politics of Modernization*. University of Chicago Press.

Awiti, Adhu. 1973. "Economic Differentiation in Ismani, Iringa Region: A Critical Assessment of Peasants' Response to the Ujamaa Vijijini Programme." *African Review* 3 (2): 209–39.

Bauer, Peter, and Basil Yamey. 1957. *The Economics of Under-developed Countries*. Chicago University Press.

Beckman, Björn. 1987. "Public Investment and Agrarian Transformation in Nigeria." In *State, Oil and Agriculture in Nigeria*, edited by Michael Watts, 110–37. University of California Press.

Bernal, Victoria. 1988. "Coercion and Incentives in African Agricultural Development: Insights from the Sudanese Experience." *African Studies Review* 31 (September): 89–108.

Bosen, J., and others. 1977. *Ugamaa: Socialism from Above*. Uppsala, Sweden: Scandinavian Institute of African Studies.

Burrows, John. 1975. *Kenya, into the Second Decade: A Report of a Mission Sent to Kenya by the World Bank*. Johns Hopkins University Press.

Callaghy, Thomas M., and John Ravenhill, eds. 1993. *Hemmed In: Responses to Africa's Economic Decline*. Columbia University Press.

Carr, Stephen. 1989. *Technology for Small-Scale Farmers in Sub-Saharan Africa*. Washington: World Bank.

Central Bank of Nigeria. 1992. *Statistical Bulletin* 3 (1).

Cleaver, Kevin M. 1993. *A Strategy to Develop Agricuture in Sub-Saharan Africa and a Focus for the World Bank*. Washington: World Bank.

Clough, Michael. 1992. *Free at Last? U.S. Policy toward Africa and the End of Cold War*. New York: Council on Foreign Relations Press.

Coleman, James S. 1958. *Nigeria: Background to Nationalism*. University of California Press.

Coulson, Andrew, ed. 1979. *African Socialism in Practice: The Tanzanian Experience*. Nottingham, U.K.: Spokesman.

Drucker, Peter F. 1986. "The Changed World Economy." *Foreign Affairs* 64 (Spring): 768-91.

European Commission. 1994. "EU-ACP Cooperation—A Special Issue." *The Courier ACP-EU*. Brussels (April).

Ewing, A. F. 1968. *Industry in Africa*. Oxford University Press.

Fadahunsi, Akin. 1979. "A Review of the Political Economy of the Industrialization Strategy of the Nigerian State, 1960-80." *African Development* 4 (August–September): 106-24.

Fallers, Lloyd A. 1956. *Bantu Bureaucracy: A Study of Integration and Conflict in the Political Institutions of an East African People*. Cambridge University Press.

Falola, Toyin, ed. 1987. *Britain and Nigeria: Exploitation or Development?* London: Zed Press.

Fieldhouse, David K. 1986. *Black Africa: Economic Decolonialization and Arrested Development*. London: George Allen and Unwin.

Fishlow, Albert. 1984. "A Summary Comment on Adelman, Balassa and Streeten." *World Development* 12 (September): 979-82.

Flammang, Robert A. 1979. "Economic Growth and Economic Development: Counterparts or Competitors?" *Economic Development and Cultural Change* 28 (October): 47-61.

Forrest, Tom. 1981. "Agricultural Policies in Nigeria, 1900-78." In *Rural Development in Tropical Africa*, edited by Judith Heyer, Pepe Roberts, and Gavin Williams, 222-258. New York: St. Martin's Press.

Forsyth, David J. C., and Robert F. Solomon. 1978. "Restrictions on Foreign Ownership of Manufacturing Industry in a Less Developed Country: The Case of Ghana." *Journal of Developing Areas* 12 (April): 281-96.

Fortmann, Louise. 1980. *Peasants, Officials and Participation in Rural Tanzania: Experience with Villagization and Decentralization*. Cornell University Center for International Studies.

Foster-Carter, Aidan. 1973. "Neo-Marxist Approaches to Development and Underdevelopment." *Journal of Contemporary Asia* 3 (1): 14-15.

———. 1978. "The Modes of Production Controversy." *New Left Review* 107 (January-February): 47-77.

———. 1987. "North Korea: The End of the Beginning." *Journal of Communist Studies* 4 (3): 64-85.

Fosu, Augustin K. 1990. "Exports and Economic Growth: The African Case." *World Development* 18 (June): 831-35.

Foxley, Alejandro. 1982. "Towards a Free Market Economy." *Journal of Development Economics* 10 (February): 3-29.

Frank, Andre G. 1967. *Capitalism and Underdevelopment in Latin America: Historical Studies of Chile and Brazil*. New York: Monthly Review Press.
————. 1975. *On Capitalist Underdevelopment*. Oxford University Press.
Franke, Richard W. 1982. *Power, Class and Traditional Knowledge in Sahel Food Production*.
Fransman, Martin, ed. 1982. *Industry and Accumulation in Africa*. London: Heinemann.
Fredericks, Leo J., Geert Kalshoven, and Jon R. V. Daane. 1980. *The Role of Farmers' Organizations in Two Paddy Farming Areas in West Malaysia*. Wageningen, Netherlands: Afdelingen voor Sociale Wetenschappen aan de Landbouwhogeschool.
Fu-Chen Lo, and Song Byung-Nak. 1979. "The Saemaul Undong: The Korean Way to Rural Transformation." Working Paper 79-09. Nagoya, Japan: United Nations Center for Regional Development.
Gakou, Mohamed. 1987. *The Crisis in African Agriculture*. London: Zed Books.
Galbraith, John Kenneth. 1979. *The Nature of Mass Poverty*. Harvard University Press.
Galenson, Alice. 1984. "Investment Incentives for Industry." Paper presented to the High-Level Seminars on Industrial Policy in Sub-Saharan Africa. World Bank, Economic Development Institute. Washington.
George, Susan. 1984. *Ill Fares the Land: Essays on Food, Hunger, Power*. Washington: Institute for Policy Studies.
————. 1992. *The Debt Boomerang: How Third World Debt Harms Us All*. Boulder, Colo.: Westview.
Gerschenkron, Alexander. 1962. *Economic Backwardness in Historical Perspective*. Cambridge: Belknap Press of Harvard University Press.
Gerster, R. 1989. "How to Ruin a Country: The Case of Togo." *Institute for Development Alternative (IFDA) Dossier* 71 (May).
Global Coalition for Africa. 1992. *Annual Report*. Washington: World Bank.
Goldin, Ian, Oden Knudsen, and Dominique van der Mensbrugghe. 1993. *Trade Liberalisation: Global Economic Implications*. OECD and World Bank.
Gulhati, Ravi, and Uday Sekhar. 1982. *Industrial Strategy for Late Starters: The Experience of Kenya, Tanzania and Zambia*. Washington: World Bank.
Hagen, Everett. 1962. *On the Theory of Social Change: How Economic Growth Begins*. Homewood, Ill.: Dorsey Press.
Heilbroner, Robert L. 1963. *The Great Ascent: The Struggle for Economic Development in Our Time*. Harper and Row.
Hirschman, Albert O. 1958. *The Strategy of Economic Development*. Yale University Press.
Husain, Ishrat, and Rashid Faruqee, eds. 1994. *Adjustment in Africa: Lessons from Country Case Studies*. Washington: World Bank.
Hyden, Göran. 1980. *Beyond Ujamaa in Tanzania: Underdevelopment and the Uncaptured Peasantry*. University of California Press.
International Bank for Reconstruction and Development. 1988. *Rural Development: World Bank Experience 1965-86*. Washington: World Bank.
International Labor Organization. 1972. *Employment, Incomes and Equality: A Strategy for Increasing Productive Employment in Kenya*. Geneva.

———. 1981. *Zambia: Basic Needs in an Economy under Pressure*. Addis Ababa, Ethiopia.

International Monetary Fund (IMF). 1988. *IMF Survey* 17 (June, Supplement on Sub-Saharan African Debt: 177–92). Washington.

———. Various years. *World Economic Outlook*. Washington.

Jaycox, E. 1992. *The Challenges of African Development*. Washington: World Bank.

Kenya, Government of. 1965. "Socialism and Its Applications to Planning in Kenya." Nairobi.

Killick, Tony. 1978. *Development Economics in Action: A Study of Economic Policies in Ghana*. New York: St. Martin's Press.

Lancaster, Carol. 1991–92. "Democracy in Africa." *Foreign Policy* 85 (Winter): 148–65.

Lerner, Daniel. 1958. *The Passing of Traditional Society: Modernizing the Middle East*. Glencoe, Ill.: Free Press.

Levy, Marion. 1952. *The Structure of Society*. Princeton University Press.

Lofchie, Michael. 1989. *The Policy Factor: Agricultural Performance in Kenya and Tanzania*. Boulder, Colo.: Rienner.

Mapolu, H. 1973. "The Social and Economic Organisation of Ujamaa Villages."

McHenry, Dean E., Jr. 1979. *Tanzania's Ujamaa Villages: The Implementation of a Rural Development Strategy*. Berkeley: University of California Institute of International Studies.

Michaels, Marguerite. 1992–93. "Retreat from Africa." *Foreign Affairs* 72 (1): 93–108.

Mkandawire, Thandinka, and Naceur Bourenane, eds. 1987. *The State and Agriculture in Africa*. Dakar, Senegal: Codesria.

Mohele, A. T. 1975. *The Ismani Maize Credit Program*. Dar es Salaam, Tanzania: University of Dar es Salaam, Economic Research Bureau.

Moore, Wilbert Ellis. 1963. *Social Change*. Englewood Cliffs, N.J.: Prentice-Hall.

Morna, Colleen Lowe. 1989. "Surviving Structural Adjustment." *Africa Report* 34 (September–October): 46–48.

Mudera, Gilbert. 1984. "The Process of Class Formation in Contemporary Zambia." In *Beyond Political Independence: Zambia's Development Predicament in the 1980s*, edited by Klass Woldring and Chibwe Chibaye, 129–59. New York: Mouton.

Nigeria, Government of. 1959. *Economic Survey of Nigeria, 1959*. Lagos: Government Printer.

———. Federal Ministry of Planning. 1981. *Outline of the Fourth National Development Plan, 1981–85*. Lagos.

Organization of African Unity (OAU). 1982. *Lagos Plan of Action for the Economic Development of Africa, 1980–2000*, 2d ed. Geneva: International Institute for Labour Studies.

———. 1985. *Africa's Priority Programme for Economic Recovery, 1986–1990*. Addis Ababa, Ethiopia.

———. 1986. *Africa's Submission to the Special Session of the United Nations General Assembly on Africa's Economic and Social Crisis*. Addis Ababa, Ethiopia.

Organski, A. F. K. 1965. *The Stages of Political Development*. New York: Knopf.

Overseas Development Institute. 1988. *Community Prices: Investing in Decline?* London.

Polsby, Nelson W. 1963. *Community Power and Political Theory*. Yale University Press.

Rustow, W. W. 1960. *The Stages of Economic Growth: A Non-Communist Manifesto*. Cambridge University Press.

———. 1971. *Politics and the Stages of Economic Growth*. Cambridge University Press.

Rweyemamu, J. F., ed. 1980. *Industrialization and Income Distribution in Africa*. Dakar, Senegal: Codesria.

Sano, Hans-Otto. 1983. *The Political Economy of Food in Nigeria, 1960–82: A Discussion on Peasants, State, and World Economy*. Uppsala, Sweden: Scandinavian Institute of African Studies.

Serageldin, Ismail. 1993. *Development Partners: Aid and Cooperation in the 1990s*. Stockholm: Swedish International Development Agency.

Shils, Edward A. 1962. *Political Development in the New States*. The Hague: Mouton.

Steel, William F., and Bassirou A. Sarr. 1983. *Agro-Industrial Development in Africa: An Overview of Trends, Policies and Institutions*. Research Memorandum 2. Abidjan, Ivory Coast: African Development Bank.

Steel, William F., and Jonathan W. Evans. 1984. *Industrialization in Sub-Saharan Africa: Strategies and Performance*. Technical paper 25. Washington: World Bank.

Tanzania, Republic of. 1964. *Statistical Abstract, 1963*. Dar es Salaam.

United Nations. 1986. *United Nations Programme of Action for African Economic Recovery and Development, 1986–1990*. New York.

———. 1991a. "Committee Evaluates African Recovery and Sets 'New Agenda.' " *UN Chronicle* 28 (December): 62–63.

———. 1991b. "In the News." *UN Chronicle*.

United Nations Conference on Trade and Development (UNCTAD). 1991. *Final Review and Appraisal of the Implementation of the United Nations Programme of Action for African Economic Recovery and Development, 1986–1990*. New York.

United Nations Economic Commission for Africa (UNECA). 1988. *The Khartoum Declaration: International Conference on the "Human Dimension of Africa's Economic Recovery and Development."* Addis Ababa, Ethiopia.

———. 1989a. *African Alternative Framework for Structural Adjustment Programmes for Socio-Economic Recovery and Transformation (AAF-SAP)*. Document E/ECA/CM, 15/6/Rev.3. Addis Ababa, Ethiopia.

———. 1989b. *Statistics and Policies: ECA Preliminary Observations on the World Bank Report, "Africa's Adjustment and Growth in the 1980's."* Addis Ababa, Ethiopia.

———. 1990. *The African Charter for Popular Participation in Development and Transformation*. Arusha, Tanzania.

United Nations Economic Social Affairs (UNESA). 1959. *Economic Survey of Africa since 1950*. Addis Ababa, Ethiopia.

Vyas, Vijay S., and Dennis Casley. 1988. *Stimulating Agricultural Growth and Rural Development in Sub-Saharan Africa.* Washington: World Bank.

World Bank. 1972. *World Development Report, 1972.* Washington.

——. 1974. *Nigeria: Options for Long-Term Development.* Johns Hopkins University Press.

——. 1981. *Accelerated Development in Sub-Saharan Africa: An Agenda for Action.* Washington.

——. 1983a. *Sub-Saharan Africa: Progress Report on Debt Prospects and Programs.* Washington.

——. 1983b. *World Tables,* 3d ed. Washington.

——1984a. *Toward Sustained Development in Sub-Saharan Africa: A Joint Program of Action.* Washington.

——. 1984b. *World Development Report, 1984.* Washington.

——. 1986–90. *Financing Growth with Adjustment in Sub-Saharan Africa.* Washington.

——. 1988. *Beyond Adjustment: Toward Sustainable Growth with Equity in Sub-Saharan Africa.* Washington.

——. 1989a. *Africa's Adjustment and Growth in the 1990s.* Washington.

——. 1989b. *Sub-Saharan Africa: From Crisis to Sustainable Growth.* Washington.

——. 1989c. *Technology for Small-Scale Farmers in Sub-Saharan Africa.* Washington.

——. 1993a. *Annual Report 1993.* Washington.

——. 1993b. *The East Asian Miracle: Economic Growth and Public Policy.* New York: Oxford University Press.

——. 1993c. *Implementing the World Bank's Strategy to Reduce Poverty: Progress and Challenges.* Washington.

——. 1993d. *A Strategy to Develop Agriculture in Sub-Saharan Africa, and a Focus for the World Bank.* Washington.

——. 1993e. *World Development Report, 1993.* Washington.

——. 1994a. *Adjustment in Africa: Reforms, Results and the Road Ahead.* Washington.

——. 1994b. *Nigeria: Structural Adjustment Program: Policies, Implementation and Impact.* Report 13053-UNI. Washington.

——. 1994c. *World Development Report, 1994.* Washington.

World Bank and U.S. Agency for International Development (USAID). 1991. *Building a Competitive Edge in Sub-Saharan African Countries: The Catalytic Role of Foreign and Domestic Enterprise Collaboration in Export Activities.* Washington.

Index